How to Own a Gun
&
Stay Out of Jail

What You Need to Know About the Law If You Own a Gun or Are Thinking of Buying One

CALIFORNIA EDITION

1997

By John Machtinger

Illustrations by Amy Wetherbee

GUN LAW PRESS
Los Angeles, California
January 1997

About the Author:

John Machtinger received his B.A. from the University of California at Berkeley and his J.D. from the University of Southern California. A practicing attorney, he has advised many Californians on gun law issues, and has become one of California's foremost authorities on gun laws.

Acknowledgments:

Thanks to Natalie Milgrim, Timothy Black, Bob Kahn, Shari Silverman, Mac Scott, Phil Newman, Shoal Hollingsworth, Dan and Bob Retting, Dan Poynter, Bruce Gordon, Shanon McClure, Stuart Ende, Jonathan Mandel, and the Machtinger family for their invaluable assistance.

Cover design: Jodi Barr

Published by:

Gun Law Press
P.O. Box 641369
Los Angeles, California 90064

Internet: jmach@netcom.com

We regret that we cannot give personal responses to legal questions.

Version 1997.1 — 10 9 8 7 6 5 4 3 2 1

Library of Congress Catalog Card Number: 95-81349

Machtinger, John F.

How to Own a Gun & Stay Out of Jail: What You Need to Know About the Law If You Own a Gun or Are Thinking of Buying One / by John Machtinger. — California 1997 ed.

ISBN 0-9642864-6-7: $9.95 Softcover

Contents

Disclaimer—Read This First

No one book covers all the laws that apply to gun owners, or all the facts of a particular situation. This book is a *summary* of selected, important laws. Read this book with the following in mind:

- ❏ This book provides general, informational material only. It does not give legal advice. Do not rely on this book to predict how the law will be applied to you or as a substitute for a lawyer.

- ❏ Laws change. This book contains the laws as they were written at the time this book was printed. It includes California and federal laws passed during 1996. When new laws are passed, they generally take effect on the next January 1, but some "urgency" legislation, as well as court decisions, can take effect immediately. It is your responsibility to keep up with changes made to the laws after this book was printed.

- ❏ Cities and counties may have their own gun laws that are not contained in this book. It is your responsibility to investigate and learn these laws on your own (see page 77).

- ❏ The author and publisher of this book are not responsible for any legal or economic result of any outcome of any situation involving guns, and are not responsible for any inadvertent errors or omissions in the reporting of the law in this book, or any changes in the law that occur after printing.

- ❏ **If a law seems vague to you as described in this book, if you don't understand it, if you are not sure whether a law applies to you, or if you have any other questions about the law or how it applies to you, consult a lawyer.**

- ❏ This book includes only California and federal laws. Do not use it as a guide to the laws of other states. This book does not contain gun laws related to hunting. Certain laws described in this book may not apply to law enforcement agencies or personnel. This book does not cover most laws that apply only to gun dealers or others in the gun business.

- ❏ This book does not assume that you are going to intentionally commit a crime. It does not discuss certain laws that would be of interest to criminals, such as sentence enhancement laws which add time to the sentences of criminals who use guns in the commission of crimes.

Terms Used in this Book

Felony: A crime punishable by death or by imprisonment in the state prison. Unless otherwise stated in the text, the punishment for a felony is 16 months, two years, or three years (many felonies carry harsher punishments). The judge decides which punishment to impose.[1]

Misdemeanor: Every crime that is not a felony or an infraction (an example of an infraction is a traffic ticket). Most gun-related misdemeanors have a punishment of up to one year in the county jail or up to a $1,000 fine, or both.[2]

Felony/Misdemeanor: A crime that can be charged or punished either as a felony or a misdemeanor. The district attorney chooses which one to charge, or the judge can decide which punishment to impose after a conviction. This type of crime is often called a "public offense" in the Penal Code, and is called a "wobbler" by people who practice criminal law. The punishment for a felony/misdemeanor is 16 months, two years, or three years in the state prison (a felony punishment), or up to one year in the county jail and/or up to a $1,000 fine (a misdemeanor punishment).[3]

DOJ: California Department of Justice.

Gun/Firearm: As used in this book, the words "gun" and "firearm" mean any device, designed to be used as a weapon, that expels a projectile through a barrel by the force of an explosion or other combustion. The terms also include the frame or receiver of a gun.[4]

Handgun: A pistol, revolver, or other gun that can be concealed upon the person (which means a gun with a barrel less than 16" in length, or that is designed to accept a barrel of less than 16").[5]

Section: Unless otherwise stated in the text, all Section numbers refer to sections of the California Penal Code.

Transfer: To sell, lease, lend, give, or in any other manner to deliver an object from you to someone else.

Endnotes

1. Penal Code §§ 17(a), (18).
2. Penal Code §§ 17(a), (19).
3. Penal Code § 18.
4. Penal Code § 12001(b), (c).
5. Penal Code § 12001(a).

Chapter 1: Who Can Buy, Own, and Possess a Gun?

Rules for Gun Purchases and Transfers

Anyone of legal age, and not in a group of persons prohibited from having a gun (discussed below), can buy one or more guns and keep them in his or her home. Guns do not need to be registered, and no permit or license is required, unless the guns are assault weapons or illegal guns. The following rules apply when you go to a gun dealer to buy a gun, or when a gun is transferred to you using the services of a gun dealer or small county sheriff's department:

Waiting Period: No gun may be delivered to you without a waiting period. During the waiting period, the DOJ checks your background to see if you are prohibited from having a gun.[1] The waiting period is 15 days for handguns and 10 days for rifles and shotguns. On April 1, 1997, the waiting period for all guns will change to 10 days (there is a possibility that the change will be delayed). The Attorney General currently adds 5 days to all gun transfers for "mailing time," extending the waiting periods by 5 days.

The waiting period starts when you fill out the paperwork for the gun purchase or transfer. If the DOJ says there is an error or omission in the paperwork or the proper fee has not been paid, the waiting period begins when all paperwork has been correctly filled out and the fee has been paid. The waiting period requirement doesn't apply to persons who have a dangerous weapon permit issued by the DOJ (see page 129).[2]

Fee for Background Check: The DOJ fee is set at $14, but may be increased annually based on the rate of inflation. The gun dealer or sheriff may pass this fee along to you; most gun dealers also add an administrative charge. If you buy or receive more than one rifle or shotgun on the same date in a single transaction, the DOJ will only charge one fee. If you buy or receive more than one handgun on the same date in a single transaction, the DOJ will charge a reduced fee for all handguns after the first one.[3]

Forms: Gun purchasers and others receiving guns must fill out a detailed form in the dealer's or sheriff department's register of sales for each gun sold or transferred. The information on the form includes your name, address, date of birth, place of birth (state or country), telephone number, occupation, sex, physical description, all legal names and aliases ever used, and your signature. You must also answer "yes" or "no" to a series of questions to determine whether you are in a group of persons who are prohibited from having a gun. The dealer must give you a copy of the completed form.[4]

Lying: If you lie about your name, address, or other information in the register of sales, or if you intentionally omit required information, you are guilty of a misdemeanor under California law. More important, if you lie to a person who has a federal firearms license (such as a gun dealer) in order to obtain a gun or ammunition, you can be fined and imprisoned for up to 10 years under federal law.[5]

Identification and Proof of Age: In order to receive a handgun, you must be at least 21 years old. In order to receive a shotgun or rifle, you must be at least 18. You must show the dealer or sheriff proof of identification and age. This proof must be either a valid California Driver's License or a California Identification Card issued by the DMV.[6]

Basic Firearms Safety Certificate: If want to buy or receive a handgun, you must have a basic firearms safety certificate unless you fall under an exception (see page 11).[7]

To receive a gun, you must show the dealer a valid California Driver's License or California Identification Card.

Basic Firearms Safety Certificates

The State Legislature believes there is a serious problem with accidental deaths and injuries, particularly among children, caused by the unsafe handling of handguns. In response, it created a program that requires people who obtain handguns to have a basic familiarity with their safe handling and storage, methods for childproofing, and the responsibilities of ownership. The program requires people who purchase or receive handguns to take *either* a 2-4 hour course *or* a short test. They are then issued a certificate which allows them to take delivery of handguns.[8]

Course: You do not have to demonstrate that you can actually use or fire handguns to complete the course and get the certificate. All you have to do is attend. In addition to the cost of the course charged by the instructor, the DOJ charges a fee of up to $10 which the instructor will collect.

Test: Most gun stores offer the test to gun buyers who need a certificate. The test is made up of between 20 and 30 written questions, and you must answer 75% right to pass. If you fail the test, you must wait 24 hours before retaking it. You can't take the test more than twice in a six-month period (if you fail the test twice, you must attend the course in order to get a certificate). If you fail the test the first time you take it, the instructor must give you additional instructional materials, such as a booklet or videotape. The second test must be taken from the same instructor that gave you the first test. The instructor may charge you a fee of up to $20, which covers taking the test up to two times and getting the certificate; $10 of this is sent to the DOJ.

You only have to take the course or pass the test once, unless you lose your certificate and do not get a duplicate certificate from the DOJ.

No Cheating: If you commit an act of "collusion" related to the basic firearms safety certificate, you are guilty of a felony/misdemeanor. "Collusion" includes answering test questions for someone else, intentionally grading the test falsely, giving an advance copy of a test to an applicant or anyone else, taking a training course or test for someone else, allowing someone to take a training course or test for someone else, and more (basically: cheating, and helping or letting an applicant cheat). If a licensed dealer commits an act of collusion, the dealer may also have his or her license revoked.[9]

Dealer Required to See Certificate: A gun dealer may not deliver a handgun to a person unless that person has a basic firearms safety certificate. A dealer can lose his or her license for violating this law.[10]

Exceptions to Certificate Requirement: Certain persons do not need a basic firearms safety certificate in order to purchase or receive a handgun, because they have already had some sort of gun training. They are:[11]

1. Licensed gun dealers.
2. Gun importers and manufacturers who are licensed under Title 18 of the United States Code, Chapter 44.
3. Active and honorably discharged members of the U.S. armed forces, national guard, air national guard, and active reserves, when they show proper identification of their involvement (such as an Armed Forces Identification Card).
4. California and federal peace officers who are authorized to carry a gun while on duty.
5. Honorably retired California peace officers listed in Sections 830.1, 830.2, and 830.5(c) (a long list).
6. Honorably retired federal officers and agents, if they were authorized to, and did, carry guns while on duty, and if they have a permit to carry a concealed weapon given by their local sheriff pursuant to Section 12027(i).
7. Persons who have a license to carry a concealed gun.
8. Persons who have a certificate of competency or a certificate of completion in hunter safety (see Fish and Game Code Section 3049 and the sections that follow). The certificate must have a hunter safety instruction validation stamp.
9. Persons who hold a valid hunting license issued by the state.
10. Persons who are authorized to carry a loaded gun under Sections 12031(c) and 12031(d) (see Chapter 2) because they have completed a course in firearms training, including patrol special police officers, zookeepers, animal control officers, harbor police officers, guards, messengers, private investigators, and patrol officers.
11. Persons who have been issued a certificate from the Department of Consumer Affairs after taking a course in firearms and arrest powers (see Section 12033).
12. Basic Firearms Safety Instructors certified by the DOJ.
13. Authorized participants in shooting matches approved by the Director of Civilian Marksmanship pursuant to the applicable provisions of Title 10 of the United States Code.
14. Persons who have successfully completed an approved peace officer training course (see Section 832).

15. Family members of police officers who have been killed in the line of duty, when receiving the officer's inoperable gun.
16. Federally-licensed collectors, who have a California certificate of eligibility, when receiving curio or relic handguns.

Prohibited Groups: People Who Can't Have a Gun

The people in the following groups can't buy, own, or possess a gun of *any kind*. Read through the following headings and subheadings. If you think you may be in one of the prohibited groups, read that section carefully. If you have been convicted of a misdemeanor in the past 10 years, pay special attention to the list that starts on page 17. Note that you can have a "conviction" on your record, and therefore be in a prohibited group, even though your sentence was suspended and you were placed on probation.[12]

Federal law applies to California gun owners; be sure to read the section on federal prohibited groups that starts on page 24. For all of these laws, a "gun" also includes the frame or receiver of a disassembled gun.[13] If you are in a prohibited group, you can't even be in possession of any part of a gun. People in prohibited groups can't possess ammunition or ammunition-related devices (such as a magazine), either.[14] If you have any doubts as to whether you are prohibited from having a gun, consult a lawyer.

Felony to Have a Gun

It is a felony for any of the following people to own a gun, possess a gun, or have a gun under their custody or control:

Convicted Felons

Anyone who has ever been convicted of a felony in California, in any other state or country, or under United States (federal) law.

If you were convicted of a crime in federal court, California law will consider you to be a convicted felon if either of the following is true: a similar offense under California law could only be punished as a felony, *or* you were sentenced to a federal correctional facility for more than 30 days or to a fine of more than $1,000, or both.[15]

Convicted as a Juvenile of Felony or 12001.6 Crime

Anyone convicted as a juvenile of a felony or a violent gun offense listed in Section 12001.6 (see list, below), if he or she was prosecuted as an adult in an adult court.[16]

Convicted of a Violent Gun Offense Listed in Section 12001.6

Anyone who has been convicted of a crime involving the violent use of a gun from the following list, whether or not the conviction was for a felony or a misdemeanor:[17]

1. Assault with a gun. An assault is an unlawful attempt to violently injure another person, when you have the ability to injure them at the time you make the attempt. (Sections 245(a)(2), 245(a)(3).)

2. Assault with a deadly weapon that is not a gun on a peace officer or firefighter in the performance of his or her duties (Section 245(c)).

3. Maliciously and willfully shooting a gun at an inhabited dwelling house or an occupied building, motor vehicle, aircraft, housecar, or camper (Section 246).

4. Drawing or brandishing a gun in a rude, angry or threatening manner in the presence of another person, or using a gun in a fight or quarrel, except in self-defense (Section 417(a)(2)). It is only a felony to have a gun after you have been convicted *a second time* of this particular offense, or if you were ever convicted of this crime as a *juvenile*. Otherwise, you can have a gun after 10 years (see below).

5. Drawing or brandishing a gun in a rude, angry or threatening manner in the immediate presence of a peace officer, when the person with the gun knows or should know that

the other person is a peace officer in the performance of his or her duties (Section 417(c)).

Once you have been convicted of a felony, you can't have a gun of any kind.

Convicted of One of 29 Serious Crimes

Anyone who has been convicted of one of the following 29 crimes, whether or not the conviction was for a felony or a misdemeanor. This includes juveniles who were tried and convicted as adults.[18]

1. Murder or voluntary manslaughter.
2. Mayhem.
3. Rape.
4. Sodomy by force, violence, duress, menace, or threat of great bodily harm.
5. Oral copulation by force, violence, duress, menace, or threat of great bodily harm.
6. Lewd acts on a child under the age of 14 years.
7. Any felony punishable by death or imprisonment in the state prison for life.
8. Any other felony in which the defendant inflicts great bodily injury on any person, other than an accomplice, which has been charged and proven, *or* any felony in which the defen-

dant uses a firearm, the use of which has been charged and proven.

9. Attempted murder.

10. Assault with intent to commit rape or robbery.

11. Assault with a deadly weapon or instrument on a peace officer.

12. Assault by a life prisoner on a noninmate.

13. Assault with a deadly weapon by an inmate.

14. Arson.

15. Exploding a destructive device or any explosive with intent to injure.

16. Exploding a destructive device or any explosive causing great bodily injury.

17. Exploding a destructive device or any explosive with intent to murder.

18. Robbery.

19. Kidnapping.

20. Taking of a hostage by an inmate of a state prison.

21. Attempt to commit a felony punishable by death or imprisonment in the state prison for life.

22. Any felony in which the defendant personally used a dangerous or deadly weapon.

23. Escape from a state prison by use of force or violence.

24. Assault with a deadly weapon or force likely to produce great bodily injury.

25. Any felony violation of Section 186.22 (participating in and helping a criminal street gang commit crimes).

26. Any attempt to commit a crime on this list other than an assault.

27. Any of the violent gun offenses in Sections 12001.6(a), (b), and (d) (see previous section).

28. Carjacking.

29. The violent gun offense in Section 12001.6(c) (threatening another person with a gun or using a gun in a fight or quarrel), *after your second conviction* for this offense (see previous section).

What's the difference between the law which makes it a felony for a convicted felon to have a gun, and this law, which makes it a felony for anyone convicted of one of 29 serious crimes to own or possess a gun?

❑ Someone who violates this law must serve at least 6 months in the county jail, even if their sentence is suspended or probation is granted, except in unusual cases. This requirement is not part of the first law (although jail time would probably result from a violation of the first law, as it is a felony).

❑ This law has an additional restriction against being able to obtain a certificate of rehabilitation, which would allow a convict to have his or her right to own a gun restored.

❑ The first law applies only to felony convictions. This law applies whether or not the person was convicted of a felony or a misdemeanor—anyone convicted of a crime on the list can't have a gun, even if he or she was only convicted of a misdemeanor.

Drug Addicts

Anyone addicted to the use of any narcotic drug. Narcotic drugs include heroin, cocaine, crack, and others. Marijuana is not a "narcotic drug" for the purposes of this law.[19]

What "addicted" means is somewhat vague. Courts have said that to be "addicted" does *not* mean the user must have withdrawal symptoms when he or she doesn't get the drug. It requires only an emotional dependence in which the user experiences a compulsive need to continue its use, along with an increased tolerance to the drug's effects which requires larger and more potent doses. The intent of this law is to stop people whose drug habits are bad enough that they would be likely to convert the possession of a gun into a crime of violence (such as armed robbery to get money to buy drugs).[20]

Even if you are not a drug addict, if you possess any amount of any substance containing cocaine, heroin, methamphetamine, or PCP while you have a loaded gun available for immediate offensive or defensive use, you are guilty of a felony punishable by two, three, or four years.[21]

Felony/Misdemeanor to Have a Gun

It is a felony/misdemeanor for the following people to own a gun, possess a gun, or have a gun under their custody or control:

Convicted of One of the Following Crimes and Having a Gun within 10 Years

Anyone who has been convicted of a *misdemeanor* violation of one of the following laws and who owns or possesses a gun, or has a gun in his or her custody or control, within 10 years of his or her conviction.[22] (Note: The section numbers listed below control your gun rights; the descriptions of the crimes are only provided for your convenience. If you have a misdemeanor conviction, check the section numbers!)

1. Threatening public officers, public employees, school officials, judges, governor's appointees, or their families with violence or property damage (Sections 71, 76).
2. Intimidating a witness with a deadly weapon (Section 136.5).
3. Threatening a witness, victim, or informant with violence or property damage (Section 140).
4. Taking a peace officer's gun while obstructing the peace officer, or attempting to do so (Section 148(d)).
5. Unlawfully bringing a weapon into a state or local public building or a public, government meeting (Section 171b).
6. Unlawfully bringing a loaded gun into a state legislative office or onto the grounds of the governor's or a state legislator's residence (Sections 171c, 171d).
7. Transferring guns to criminal street gang members (Section 186.28).

Many misdemeanor convictions can cause you to lose your right to have a gun for 10 years, including assault, battery, brandishing a gun, and having a gun in a school or government building.

8. Assault (Sections 240, 241). An assault is an unlawful attempt to violently injure another person, when you have the ability to injure them at the time you make the attempt.

9. Battery (Sections 242, 243). A battery is any willful and unlawful use of force or violence upon another person.

10. Assault with a Taser or a stun gun (Section 244.5). A Taser is a device which shoots electrified metal barbs.

11. Assault with a deadly weapon or with force likely to produce great bodily injury (Sections 245, 245.5).

12. Maliciously and willfully shooting a gun at an inhabited dwelling house or an occupied building, motor vehicle, aircraft, housecar, or camper (Section 246).

13. Willfully discharging a gun in a grossly negligent manner which could cause injury or death to another person (Section 246.3).

14. Willfully shooting at an unoccupied aircraft; or, at an unoccupied motor vehicle, an uninhabited dwelling house, or an uninhabited building, without the permission of the owner (Section 247).

15. Willfully inflicting corporal injury (a beating that causes any physical injury) on a spouse, live-in lover, or the person with whom one has had children (Section 273.5).

16. Willful violation of a court order to prevent domestic violence or disturbance of the peace (Section 273.6).

17. Drawing or brandishing a gun in a rude, angry or threatening manner in the presence of another person, or using a gun in a fight or quarrel, except in self defense (Sections 417, 417.1). If you have two or more convictions for violating Section 417(a)(2), or if you were convicted of this crime as a juvenile, possession of a gun becomes a felony.

18. Purchasing, selling, manufacturing, shipping, transporting, distributing, or receiving imitation firearms (guns that look real but can't fire) in violation of the rules in Section 417.2.

19. Inflicting serious bodily injury while drawing or brandishing a gun in a rude, angry, or threatening manner, except in self-defense (Section 417.6).

20. Bringing or possessing a gun on the grounds of any public or private school, community college, or university, or having a gun in a school zone (Section 626.9).

21. Stalking (Section 646.9). Stalking is willfully, maliciously, and repeatedly following or harassing a person to make that person fear for their safety or the safety of their family.

22. Carrying a loaded gun with the intent to commit a felony (Section 12023).

23. Possessing a deadly weapon with the intent to commit an assault (Section 12024).

24. Willfully and maliciously discharging a gun from a motor vehicle, or being the driver of a motor vehicle and allowing another occupant to do so (Sections 12034(b), (d)).

25. Carrying a gun while masked to hide your identity (Section 12040).

26. Gun dealer transferring a gun to an underage person (Section 12072(b)).

27. Unlawfully transferring a gun to a prohibited person, to a minor, or to a straw buyer; buying a gun as a straw buyer; cheating on a basic firearms safety certificate test; unlawfully transferring a handgun without using a gun dealer. (See Section 12072(g)(3) for list of section numbers).

28. Selling a pistol, revolver, or other concealable gun to a minor (former Section 12100(a)).

29. Unauthorized possession of a machinegun (Section 12220).

30. Possessing any metal- or armor-piercing handgun ammunition (Section 12320).

31. Picketing (or otherwise engaging in an organized refusal to work) in a public place while carrying a concealed or loaded gun or a deadly weapon, or while wearing the uniform of a peace officer (Section 12590).

32. Bringing a gun into a Youth Authority or county juvenile facility (Welfare & Inst. Code Sections 871.5, 1001.5).

33. Transferring a gun to a prohibited person with a mental disorder (Welfare & Institutions Code Section 8101).

34. Possession of a gun by a prohibited mentally ill person (Welfare & Institutions Code Sections 8100, 8103).

Prohibited by Probation

Any person who, as an express condition of probation, is prohibited or restricted from owning, possessing, controlling, receiving, or purchasing a firearm. This law applies if the person is not already subject to one the other prohibitions on having a gun.[23]

Juvenile Convict Who Has Gun Before Age 30

Any person who, as a juvenile, committed an offense listed in Welfare and Institutions Code Section 707(b), or in Penal Code Section 1203.073, or a misdemeanor from the list that begins on page 17, was made a ward of the juvenile court, and who owns or possesses a gun before the age of 30 years. In other words, these people can't have a gun until they turn 30.[24]

The offenses listed in Welfare and Institutions Code 707(b) are generally violent crimes, ranging from murder to armed robbery to sexual abuse, although making or selling certain amounts of cocaine products and bribing a witness are on the list. Penal Code Section 1203.073 lists various drug crimes involving the manufacture, possession for sale, sale, and transport of cocaine, cocaine base, methamphetamine, PCP, and heroin (as well as certain related crimes, such as having a minor assist in the manufacture, transport, etc.). The list that begins on page 17 consists of violent and gun-related misdemeanors. If you are unsure whether you are in this group (or any other), look up the code sections and/or consult a lawyer.

Protective Order with Gun Restriction

Any person who purchases or receives (gets) a gun, or attempts to do so, knowing that he or she is subject to a protective order issued by a court under the Family Code or under the Code of Civil Procedure prohibiting him or her from owning or getting a gun. These orders are restraining orders that keep someone away from a residence, that prohibit acts of abuse or other acts, or that prohibit the harassment of co-workers.

For this prohibition against getting a gun to apply, the restraining order must have been personally served on the person and must contain a statement in bold print of the gun restriction and of the penalties for violation; *or*, the court must have given oral notice of the gun restriction and penalties to the restrained person. The prohibition does not prevent a person from receiving a gun as part of a community property disposition (divorce).[25]

New in 1995, the court may also order a person subject to a protective order issued under the Family Code to surrender (turn in) any guns he or she already has until the protective order ends. See Family Code Section 6389 for details.

Persons with Certain Mental Disorders

Dangerous Inpatients: Persons admitted to a facility with or without their consent and who, in the opinion of the attending health care professional, are a danger to self or others as specified by Welfare and Institutions Code Sections 5150, 5250, or 5300. The prohibition ends when the person is discharged from the facility. A leave of absence is not considered a discharge.[26]

Psychotic Person Admitted to Facility or Certified for Intensive Treatment—No Gun For 5 Years: Any person who is arrested under Welfare & Institutions Code Section 5150 because he or she is a danger to self or others, and then evaluated and admitted to a facility under Welfare & Institutions Sections 5151 and 5152, can't have a gun for *five years* after he or she is released from the facility. Also, any person certified for intensive treatment under Welfare & Institutions Code Sections 5250, 5260, or 5270.15 can't have a gun for five years. If the person wants a gun before the five years is up, the person can ask the superior court to rule that he or she is likely to use a gun in a safe and lawful manner. See Welfare & Institutions Code Section 8103(f).[27]

Threat Communicated to Psychotherapist—No Gun for 6 Months: A person who has communicated to a licensed psychotherapist[28] a serious threat of physical violence against a person, can't have a gun for a period of *six months from the time the psychotherapist makes a report* of the threat to the police. The person who made the threat will receive a notice from the DOJ that he or she is prohibited from possessing a gun for six months. The person can go to court to get the prohibition removed. The law *requires* a therapist to make a report to the police if the threat is serious and the potential victim(s) can be identified.[29]

Court-Declared Mental Disorder or Sex Offender: Any person who was adjudicated (declared) by a court of any state after October 1, 1955 to be a danger to others as a result of a mental disorder or mental illness, or who was adjudicated to be a mentally disordered sex offender. If the same court later gives the person a certificate that he or she can have a gun without endangering others, the prohibition is lifted (unless the person is again declared to be mentally disordered or a sex offender after getting the certificate).[30]

22

Found Not Guilty by Reason of Insanity: Any person who has been found not guilty by reason of insanity by any state or federal court in the United States of any of a long list of violent or dangerous crimes, including felonies involving death, great bodily injury, the threat of bodily harm to another person, and others. See Welfare & Institutions Code Sections 8103(b), (c) and Penal Code Section 1026.

Any person who was found not guilty by reason of insanity of any other crime is also prohibited from having a gun. However, if their crime is not on the list in Section 8103(b), they can regain their right to have a gun if the court of commitment finds that the they have recovered their sanity. See Penal Code Section 1026.2 for details.[31]

Found Mentally Incompetent to Stand Trial: Any person who has been found mentally incompetent to stand trial, unless the committing court has restored the person's competence to stand trial. See Welfare & Institutions Code Section 8103(d) and Penal Code Sections 1370 and 1370.1.

Placed Under Conservatorship because of Mental Disorder or Alcoholism: Any person who has been placed under conservatorship by any court in the United States, state or federal, because the person is gravely disabled as a result of a mental disorder or impairment by chronic alcoholism. The prohibition only applies if the court ruled that the person would present a danger to self or others if he or she had a gun. The court must notify the person of the gun prohibition. The prohibition ends when the conservatorship ends.[32]

Confiscation of Guns Possessed by Mentally Disordered Persons: Whenever a person is in one of the above groups, or is arrested or detained for a mental examination, the police can confiscate any guns possessed by that person. After taking a gun, the police will notify the person of the procedure to get the gun back. See Welfare & Institutions Code Section 8102 for details.[33]

Federal Offense to Have a Gun

Federal law has its own prohibited groups. It's a federal crime for any of the following people to have a gun or ammunition. The penalty for violation is much harsher than California law: a fine and up to ten years in a federal penitentiary.[34]

- ❑ **Persons Convicted of a Crime Punishable by More Than One Year:** Anyone who has been convicted of a state or federal crime punishable by imprisonment for more than one year (no matter what punishment the person actually received). These crimes do not include state misdemeanors punishable by two years or less. They also do not include certain business crimes such as antitrust or unfair trade practices.

- ❑ **Fugitives from Justice.**

- ❑ **Drug Users or Addicts:** Anyone who is an *unlawful user* or addict of a controlled substance, *including marijuana,* cocaine, heroin, all other illegal drugs, and prescription drugs that are regulated because they have a potential for abuse.[35]

- ❑ **Mental Patients:** Anyone who has been adjudicated (ruled by a court) to be a mental defective or who has been committed to a mental institution.

- ❑ **Illegal Aliens.**

- ❑ **Persons Dishonorably Discharged from the Armed Forces.**

- ❑ **Persons Who Renounced (Gave Up) Their U.S. Citizenship.**

- ❑ **Persons Under a Restraining Order** that restrains them from harassing, stalking, or threatening an "intimate partner" or the intimate partner's child. See Title 18 of the United States Code, Section 921(g) for details.

❑ **Persons Convicted of a Domestic Violence Misdemeanor** involving any violence or threat against anyone he or she has lived with or had children with. If this ban might apply to you, see 18 United States Code, Section 921(a)(33)(A) for important details, or consult a lawyer. Federal law provides ways for you to restore your right to have a gun. This new law is under challenge, and may be changed. Remember that the California 10-year prohibition may still apply (see page 17).

❑ **Employees** of any of the above persons when they have a gun as part of their employment.

❑ **Persons Under Indictment for a Crime Punishable by More Than 1 Year:** These persons are not prohibited from keeping a gun they already have at the time the charges are filed, but after charges are filed they can't receive (get) any gun or ship or transport any gun.[36]

Federal law has its own set of prohibited groups which apply to people who have guns in California.

25

If You're in a Prohibited Group, Can You Ever Have Your Gun Rights Restored?

Several of the prohibited groups only restrict a group member from having a gun for a limited period of time. For example, a drug user can have a gun again when he or she no longer uses drugs. Someone who can't have a gun for 10 years after certain misdemeanor convictions can have a gun again 10 years after his or her conviction.

If you are in a prohibited group whose gun ban does not automatically end at a certain point in time, or if you want a gun within 10 years after you have been convicted of one of the qualifying misdemeanors, there are some limited ways you can get your right to have a gun restored:

❑ **Felony—Dangerous Weapon Used:** If you were convicted of a felony that involved the use of a dangerous weapon (including a gun), you will probably never be able to legally have a gun. California law doesn't allow any sort of pardon or certificate of rehabilitation for someone in this position.[37] The only way to have a gun again would be to get a "full and unconditional" pardon from the President of the United States. This type of pardon would restore your gun rights.[38]

❑ **Felony—No Dangerous Weapon Used:** If you were convicted of a felony that did *not* involve the use of a gun or a dangerous weapon, there is a procedure for you to apply to have your gun rights restored. See Penal Code Sections 4852.01 (and the sections that follow) and 4852.17 for details.[39]

❑ **Misdemeanor From List:** If you were convicted of a misdemeanor from the list that starts on page 17, there are two ways to restore your right to have a gun before the 10-year period is up. If you were convicted before 1991 or before your violation was placed on the 10-year list, you can petition the court for relief from the prohibition on having a gun. See Sections 12021(c)(3), (4) for detailed rules, and see the court case *In Re Evans* (1996) 49 Cal.App.4th 1263, 1274.

If you are a peace officer whose employment depends on having a gun, and you were convicted of corporal injury, disobeying a protective order, or stalking, you can petition the court to restore your gun rights. See Section 12021(c).

❑ **Emergencies:** When you are in a prohibited group, you can still obtain a gun in an emergency situation, in order to protect your life or safety or the life or safety of another person. See page 105 for details.

❑ **Federal Law:** If you are in a prohibited group under federal law, you can apply for the right to have a gun again. See Title 18 of the United States Code, Section 925(c), for the procedure. If you were convicted of a state crime punishable by more than 1 year in prison, you automatically can have a gun again under federal law when the convicting state restores your right to have a gun by pardoning you, restoring your civil rights, or expunging or setting aside your conviction.

If you believe you were wrongly convicted of a crime, you must have your conviction overturned in the court that convicted you *before* you get a gun.[40] If you were convicted in another state, you must have your right to have a gun restored in that state before you may have a gun in California.[41] *And*, you may also have to have your rights restored under California law. Consult a lawyer. The bottom line: If you have a conviction and don't know whether you are now in a prohibited group, or don't know whether your gun rights were restored, consult a lawyer *before* getting a gun.

When Can a Minor Have a Gun?

A minor is someone under 18 years of age (federal gun laws call them "juveniles").[42] Both California and federal laws govern when a minor can have a gun or ammunition. In addition to the laws discussed below, remember that *all* gun laws apply to minors. Some cities and counties have laws that restrict minors from possessing guns and ammunition. See the section that starts on page 77 for details on how to learn these laws.

Handguns: Federal Law

The federal crime bill passed in 1994 adds new restrictions on when a minor can have a handgun or handgun ammunition. Federal law now bans possession by minors, and bans the transfer of a handgun or handgun ammunition by any person to a minor, but there are several exceptions.

Under federal law, it is illegal for a minor to knowingly possess a handgun or ammunition that can only be used in a handgun. Violation is punishable by probation for minors with clean records, and by a fine and up to one year in prison for others. It's also illegal for any person to sell, deliver, or otherwise transfer a handgun or handgun ammunition to a minor. Violation is punishable by a fine and up to one year in prison (and by up to 10 years in prison if the person who transfers the gun knows the minor intends to use the gun in a crime of violence).[43]

This law does *not* apply to:

❏   A *temporary* transfer of a handgun and ammunition to a minor when the minor is using it: for target practice, for hunting, for handgun use and safety instruction, in the course of employment, or in the course of ranching or farming at the minor's residence or at another ranch or farm with the rancher's or farmer's permission. All the rules listed below must be followed:

1. The minor must have the prior *written* consent of his or her parent or legal guardian. The parent or guardian must not be in a group of people who are prohibited from having a gun. The minor must have this written consent in his or her possession at all times when in possession of the gun or ammunition.

2. The minor must transport the handgun unloaded in a locked container when going to or from the activity, and must follow all state and local gun laws.

3. Ranching or farming use must be done under the direction of an adult who is not in a group of people who are prohibited from having a gun.

❑ A minor in the U.S. Armed Forces or the National Guard, who has a handgun in the line of duty.

❑ A minor who inherits legal title to a handgun or ammunition, but who does not possess them.

❑ A minor who takes possession of a handgun and ammunition in order to defend himself, herself, or other people against an intruder in the minor's home or a home where the minor is an invited guest.

Handguns: California Law

It is illegal for a minor in California to possess a handgun. There are four situations where this law does *not* apply:[44]

❑ The minor is accompanied by his or her parent or legal guardian.

❑ The minor is accompanied by a "responsible adult," and has the prior *written* consent of his or her parent or legal guardian. A "responsible adult" is someone over 21 who is not in a group of persons who are prohibited from having a gun.

❑ The minor is at least 16 years old, and has the prior *written* consent of his or her parent or legal guardian.

29

❑ The minor has the prior *written* consent of his or her parent or legal guardian, and is on lands owned or lawfully possessed his or her parent or legal guardian.

"Lawful Recreational Sport:" In order for the above exceptions to apply, the minor must be actively engaged in, or going directly to or from, a "lawful, recreational sport." Lawful, recreational sports include: competitive shooting; agricultural, ranching, and hunting activities; entertainment and theatrical productions or events; and other lawful, recreational sports. To qualify, the nature of the activity must involve the use of a gun.

Minors who possess a handgun in violation of this law are guilty of a misdemeanor if they have a clean record, and of a felony/misdemeanor if they have previously been convicted of violating this law or certain other laws.

Any person who transfers a handgun to a minor is guilty of a felony/misdemeanor. This law does *not* apply to:[45]

❑ The loan of a handgun to a minor by the minor's parent or legal guardian if the minor is being loaned the gun to engage in a lawful, recreational sport (see definition, above), and the duration of the loan is no longer than reasonably necessary for the minor to engage in that activity.

❑ The loan of a handgun to a minor by a person who is not the minor's parent or legal guardian if:

1. The minor has the written consent of his or her parent or legal guardian, and this consent is presented to the person loaning the gun before or at the time the loan is made; or, if the minor is accompanied by his or her parent or legal guardian at the time the loan is made;

2. The minor is loaned the gun to engage in a lawful, recreational sport (see definition, above); and

3. The duration of the loan is no longer than reasonably necessary for the minor to engage in that activity, and in no case is longer than 10 days.

Detailed federal and state rules govern when you can give a gun or ammunition to a minor.

Rifles and Shotguns

Any person who transfers a rifle or shotgun to a minor is guilty of a misdemeanor. There are two exceptions to this law:[46]

❑ The transfer or loan of a rifle or shotgun to a minor by the minor's parent or legal guardian, or by the minor's grandparent with the express permission of the minor's parent or legal guardian.

❑ The loan of a rifle or shotgun to a minor by another person with the express permission of the minor's parent or legal guardian, if the loan does not exceed 30 days and is for a lawful purpose.

Ammunition

It is illegal for a minor in California to possess live ammunition for any type of gun. This law does *not* apply in the following three situations:[47]

❑ The minor has the *written* consent of his or her parent or legal guardian to possess live ammunition.

❑ The minor is accompanied by his or her parent or legal guardian.

❑ The minor is engaged in or going directly to or from a "lawful, recreational sport" (see page 30).

A first conviction for violating this law for a minor with a clean record is a misdemeanor. A minor who has previously been convicted of violating this law or certain other laws is guilty of a felony/misdemeanor.

Any person who sells ammunition or ammunition-related devices (such a a magazine) to a minor, knowing the minor's age, is guilty of a misdemeanor.[48]

Other Rules and Examples

BB and Paint Guns: A minor can possess a "BB device" only with the permission of his or her parent. A BB device is any instrument which expels a metallic projectile such as a BB or pellet through air pressure, CO_2 pressure, or spring action; it also includes paint guns. Any person who sells a BB device to a minor, or who furnishes (gives or lends) a BB device to a minor without the express or implied permission of the minor's parent or legal guardian, is guilty of a misdemeanor.[49]

Examples of "Express" and "Implied" Permission: "Express" permission would be a written or oral statement that the minor can possess a gun, such as, "It is OK for Junior to have a .22 caliber rifle." "Implied" permission would be a statement such as, "When you go on the camping trip, make sure Junior wears eye protection when he shoots your BB gun." That statement implies that the parent gave permission for Junior to possess your BB gun, even though the parent didn't say it directly.

Comment for Parents: If you are considering letting your child have a gun, for target practice, hunting, or other reasons, you should keep the following in mind:

If you give your child a handgun or any type of live ammunition to use without your being present, write down on a sheet of paper, "I, _____ (your name), am the parent (or legal guardian) of _____ (child's name). I give permission for _____ (child's name) to possess the following gun: _____ (make, model, and caliber of gun), as well as live ammunition for it." Then sign your name, print your name below your signature, and write the date. Give this to your child to have in his or her possession when he or she has the gun or ammunition. This should satisfy the "written consent" requirement for handguns and ammunition (make sure you follow all the other requirements).

Your child should be trained in gun safety and handling by a competent instructor. Before you give your child a gun to use without your direct supervision, carefully consider your decision. If your child is using the gun without you around and kills or injures someone, you will almost certainly be sued by the victim's family (even if you are present, you could still be sued).

Endnotes

1. Penal Code §§ 12072(c)(1), 12071(b)(3)(a).
2. Penal Code §§ 12072(c)(1), 12071(b)(3)(A), 12078(r).
3. Penal Code §§ 12076(d), (e), (g), (h); 12084(d)(5), (6).
4. Penal Code §§ 12077(a), 12076(b)(3).
5. Penal Code § 12076(a); 18 U.S.C. §§ 922(a)(6), 924(a)(2).
6. Penal Code §§ 12072(b), (c)(3), 12071(b)(3)(C), (c)(1).
7. Penal Code § 12072(c)(5).

8. Penal Code § 12800, et seq.
9. Penal Code §§ 12072(e), (g)(3)(H), 12071(b)(10).
10. Penal Code §§ 12071(b)(8), 12072(b)(5).
11. Penal Code § 12081.
12. People v. Loomis (1965) 231 Cal.App.2d 594, 597.
13. Penal Code § 12001(c).
14. Penal Code § 12316(b).
15. Penal Code § 12021(a), (f).
16. Penal Code § 12021(b).
17. Penal Code §§ 12021(a), 12001.6; *See also* § 12021.1(b)(27).
18. Penal Code § 12021.1.
19. Penal Code § 12021(a); Health & Safety Code § 11019.
20. People v. Washington (1965) 237 Cal.App.2d 59, 68.
21. Health & Safety Code § 11370.1.
22. Penal Code § 12021(c)(1).
23. Penal Code § 12021(d).
24. Penal Code § 12021(e).
25. Penal Code § 12021(g); *See also* Family Code §§ 6218, 6304, Code of Civil Procedure §§ 527.6, 527.8.
26. Welfare & Institutions Code § 8100(a),(c).
27. Welfare & Institutions Code § 8103(f),(g).
28. *See* Evidence Code § 1010(a)-(e).
29. Welfare & Institutions Code §§ 8100(b), 8105(c).
30. Welfare & Institutions Code § 8103(a).
31. Welfare & Institutions Code § 8103(c).
32. Welfare & Institutions Code § 8103(e).
33. Welfare & Institutions Code § 8102.
34. 18 U.S.C. § 922(g), (h).
35. *See* 21 U.S.C. § 802.
36. 18 U.S.C. § 922(n).
37. People v. Ratcliff (1990) 223 Cal.App.3d 1401, 1409-1410.
38. Bradford v. Cardoza (1987) 195 Cal.App.3d 361, 365.
39. Helmer v. Miller (1993) 19 Cal.App.4th 1565, 1570.
40. People v. Harty (1985) 173 Cal.App.3d 493, 500.
41. United States v. Eaton (9th cir. 1994) 94 D.A.R. 10432.
42. Family Code § 6500; 18 U.S.C. § 922(x)(5).
43. 18 U.S.C. §§ 922(x), 924(a)(5).
44. Penal Code § 12101(a), (c).
45. Penal Code §§ 12072(a)(3), (g)(3)(A), 12078(p)(2), (3).
46. Penal Code §§ 12072(a)(3), (g)(1), 12078(p)(1), (4), (5).
47. Penal Code § 12101(b), (c).
48. Penal Code § 12316(a), (b)(2).
49. Penal Code §§ 12551, 12552, 12001(g).

Chapter 2: When Can You Carry Concealed or Loaded Guns?

Overview

There are two main laws that govern when you may carry your gun on your person or in your motor vehicle. The first is Penal Code Section 12025, which prohibits carrying a concealed handgun on your person or in your vehicle. This book refers to Section 12025 as the "concealed gun law" (many people refer to this as the law against "carrying a concealed weapon"). The second law is Penal Code Section 12031, which prohibits carrying any loaded gun in a public place or on a public street. This book refers to Section 12031 as the "loaded gun law."

Both these laws have numerous exceptions, which are discussed below. The most important exception is the one that allows you to have a concealed and loaded gun in your home. If you carry a concealed and/or loaded gun and do *not* fall under any of the exceptions, you can be charged with two misdemeanors (or worse, if you have prior convictions), and if you are convicted, you could go to jail.

How to Read this Chapter: First read the section on the concealed gun law. Next, read the section on the loaded gun law. Think about them for a moment, and make sure you understand what type of behavior each law is meant to control. Then, read through the different exceptions starting on page 42, and mark any that apply to you. Also, read Chapter 3 on which places have "extra" restrictions on guns. This will give you an idea of where you can and can't have your gun. If you have any doubts about how any of the laws apply to you, research the laws, contact your local police, and/or consult a lawyer.

Concealed Gun Law (Section 12025)

The "concealed gun law" prohibits you from carrying a concealed (hidden) pistol or revolver on your person or in your motor vehicle. In addition to pistols and revolvers, it applies to all other "concealable" guns, which means guns that can fit a barrel less than 16" in length, and to flare guns and other rocket-propelled projectiles.[1]

Here is the main part of Section 12025, word for word. Read it carefully:

"(a) A person is guilty of carrying a concealed firearm when he or she does any of the following:

(1) Carries concealed within any vehicle which is under his or her control or direction any pistol, revolver, or other firearm capable of being concealed upon the person.

(2) Carries concealed upon his or her person any pistol, revolver, or other firearm capable of being concealed upon the person."

What this Means: Unless you fall under one of the exceptions, you cannot carry a handgun (or any other concealable gun or flare gun) that is:

1. Hidden in your car, such as in the glove box, in the door compartment, under the seat, or in a bag in the car. Even if you don't own the car, if you are in control of the car you are responsible for any gun that you know is hidden in it.

2. Hidden on your person, such as in a holster hidden under your clothing or in the waistband of your pants.

3. In your purse, briefcase, or knapsack. You "carry" a gun on your person or in your vehicle when the movement of the person or the vehicle carries the gun along with it.[2]

❑ For the concealed gun law, *it does not matter whether the gun is loaded*, so long as it is a hidden gun.

The concealed gun law applies even to unloaded guns. Carrying a handgun in a purse, briefcase, or knapsack is the same as carrying it in your waistband—it's a gun concealed "on your person."

"Concealed" Applies to Any Part of the Gun

The word "concealed" has been given a very broad meaning by California courts. If *any part* of the gun is concealed, *even just the clip*, the gun can be considered a concealed gun.

Courts have gone so far as to think of a gun's clip as being a "part" of the gun. In general, even if a gun has been disassembled into two or more parts it's still a "gun" in the eyes of the law. Courts have applied this theory to the concealed gun law, and consider a hidden clip to be a partially concealed gun.[3]

Because the concealed gun law applies only to guns that are partially or totally hidden, you may carry your unloaded handgun in your car as long as all its parts are in plain view.[4] This practice is *not* recommended. You may end up looking down the wrong end of a police officer's gun if you are pulled over while carrying your gun in this manner.

Loaded Gun Law (Section 12031)

The "loaded gun law" prohibits you from carrying a loaded gun of any kind (handgun, rifle, shotgun, etc.) on most public streets and in most public places. It also applies to flare guns and other rocket-propelled projectiles.[5] Here is the main part of Section 12031, word for word. Read it carefully:

"(a)(1) Every person who carries a loaded firearm on his or her person or in a vehicle while in any public place or on any public street in an incorporated city or in any public place or on any public street in a prohibited area of unincorporated territory is guilty of a misdemeanor."

What this Means: Unless you fall under one of the exceptions, you cannot carry a loaded handgun, rifle, shotgun, or any other loaded gun:

1. On your person or in your vehicle...

2. ...when you are in most public places and on most public streets.

3. Whether or not it is concealed does not matter.

4. Whether or not it is in your trunk does not matter.

5. Whether or not it is in a locked container does not matter.

6. Whether or not you know it's loaded does not matter.

What Is a "Loaded Gun?"

According to the Penal Code, a gun is "loaded" when there is an unfired cartridge (some people call this a "bullet") or shotgun shell *attached in any manner* to the gun. This includes cartridges and shells in the firing chamber, and in the magazine or clip if that magazine or clip is attached to the gun. A muzzle-loader gun is "loaded" when it is capped or primed, and has a powder charge and ball or shot in the barrel or cylinder.

In 1996, the California Court of Appeal clarified the phrase "attached in any manner." To be "loaded," the court said, a gun must have ammunition in a position where it is *ready for firing*. Ammunition in a magazine or clip is considered ready for firing. But ammunition only in a storage space, such as the stock of a rifle or shotgun, is not. Thus, the rule is that a gun is "loaded" when there is ammunition attached in any manner to the gun, if that ammunition is also in a position where it is ready for firing.[6]

The law is not clear on whether you can carry a loaded magazine in the same container as the gun it fits into without falling under the loaded gun law. The answer depends on whether a magazine in the same container is "attached" to the gun. Carry both in the same container at your own risk!

There is no requirement that when you have a gun in your car you must keep the gun in the trunk and the ammunition in the glove box. However, keeping the gun and ammunition in separate parts of the car might help you prove to a police officer or court that you are not violating the loaded gun law.

Whether or not you *know* the gun is loaded does not matter. If it's loaded and you're in a place where loaded guns are not permitted, and no exception applies, you have violated the loaded gun law.

Example

Appellate Court Case: People v. Dillard. Dillard had lent his .30-30 Winchester rifle to his stepfather several times to use hunting. Each time, his stepfather had returned the rifle unloaded. One June morning, Dillard was riding his bicycle home on an Oakland street after picking up the rifle from his stepfather. He was carrying the rifle in a rifle case. An Oakland Police officer stopped Dillard and examined the rifle. It had one round of ammunition inside the chamber and six additional rounds inside the magazine. Dillard was found guilty by a jury of the misdemeanor offense of carrying a loaded gun on his person in a public place.

Dillard appealed, arguing that he should have been allowed to introduce evidence at his trial that he didn't know the rifle was loaded. The court disagreed, saying that knowledge that a gun is loaded is not part of the offense of carrying a loaded gun in a public place. It's the duty of every person carrying a gun to check to see whether the gun is loaded, the court said. Dillard lost his appeal.[7]

What Are a "Public Place" and a "Public Street?"

A "public place" is any place where the public normally has access. An example is the parking lot of a supermarket.[8] Even though it's private property, the public goes there to shop at the market. "Public place" is a very broad term.

A "public street" is simply any street, road, or highway that's not on private property.

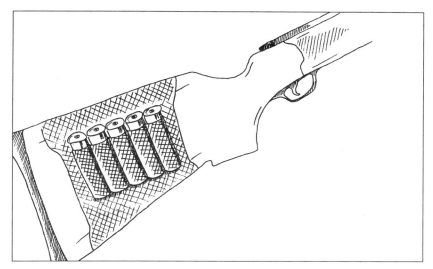

The ammunition attached to this shotgun stock does not by itself make the gun "loaded."

Which Public Places and Public Streets Are Covered by the Loaded Gun Law?

Inside city limits (inside an "incorporated city"), the loaded gun law applies in all public places and on all public streets.

Outside city limits (in "unincorporated territory," which is land that's inside a county but outside a city), the loaded gun law applies in all "prohibited areas." A prohibited area is any place where it's illegal to shoot a gun.[9]

Exactly where it's illegal to shoot a gun is somewhat unclear. The simple answer is this: Most counties have ordinances that prohibit shooting a gun except in a designated shooting area. Designated shooting areas are outdoor places where you can practice shooting. Their locations are listed in your local county code, or contact your local sheriff's department. In these counties, the loaded gun law applies in all places except designated shooting areas. (Your county may be different. See your county code or contact your county sheriff.) You should assume that the loaded gun law

41

applies in every public place and on every public street in California, unless you are in a designated shooting area.

Police Can Search Without Warrant

If a law enforcement officer sees you carrying a gun on your person or in your vehicle (including the trunk) while in any place where a loaded gun is prohibited, the officer can examine the gun to determine whether it's loaded. If you refuse to allow the officer to inspect the gun, your refusal gives the officer probable cause to arrest you for violating the loaded gun law (this does not mean you're automatically guilty; it means that the officer can arrest you even though he or she is not sure about whether you have committed a crime).[10]

Comment: If a law enforcement officer asks you for permission to conduct any type of search, and you do not wish to consent (give permission) to the search, tell the officer clearly that you do not consent to the search. You have a right not to give your consent. But *never* put up any physical resistance to a search by a law enforcement officer.

Basic Exceptions to the Concealed and Loaded Gun Laws

There are many exceptions to the concealed gun law and the loaded gun law. Here is a simple way you can sort them out so you don't get lost: Each time you want to have a concealed handgun, and each time you want to have a loaded gun in a public place or on a public street, you have to fall under an exception.

If you want to carry a concealed handgun on your person in your house, you need an exception that allows you to do that. If you want to have a loaded gun in your place of business, you need an exception. If you want to transport a handgun in your car, you need an exception to do that, too. If you want to carry a loaded gun or a concealed handgun on the street, you need another exception. Some exceptions are only exceptions to the concealed gun law, some are only for the loaded gun law, and some are for both. *You don't need a permit or license for any of these exceptions unless an exception states that you do.*

Read each exception carefully before deciding whether it applies to you. If you don't think one applies, it probably doesn't. You won't have much luck convincing the district attorney not to prosecute you for carrying a concealed gun if you claim, for example, that you and your shooting buddy have a "shooting club" (see Shooting Clubs exception), and that you were going to the "target range" which just happens to be at his house, unless this is obviously true.

Rifles and Shotguns

Exception to the Concealed Gun Law: Yes.

Exception to the Loaded Gun Law: No.

The concealed gun law does not apply to rifles and shotguns because they are not "concealable" guns (unless they can accept a barrel less than 16" in length). The loaded gun law applies to *all* guns. This means that you can transport or carry your rifle or shotgun in your car or on your person, openly or hidden, anywhere. However, it can't be loaded or have ammunition attached to it while you are in a public place or on a public street, unless another exception applies.

Reasonable Belief of Immediate, Grave Danger

Exception to the Concealed Gun Law: No.

Exception to the Loaded Gun Law: Yes.

You may carry a loaded (but not concealed) gun if you *reasonably* believe: (1) that you or your property is in immediate, grave danger, *and* (2) that you must carry a loaded gun in order to protect your safety or your property. You may also carry a loaded gun in order to protect the safety of another person or that person's property.[11]

You can only carry the loaded gun during the *brief interval* before and after you have had a chance to call the local law enforcement agency and notify them of the danger, and before officers have arrived to assist you. You must call for help as soon as it is reasonably possible.

If you are tried for violating the loaded gun law, the jury (or judge, if you do not have a jury trial) will decide whether a person in your situation would reasonably have believed himself or herself to be in grave danger and whether you acted reasonably. What's "reasonable" is based on what the average prudent (wise) person would do.

The Reasonable Belief of Immediate, Grave Danger exception lets you defend yourself on the street with a gun.

Comment: This exception applies everywhere, including on the street. If you reasonably believe there is an immediate, grave (very serious) danger, you may carry a loaded gun to protect a person's safety. Before the danger is present, your gun must be carried legally, such as unloaded in a locked container. After it's loaded, no part of the gun can be concealed. You must call the police or sheriff as soon as you safely can. You can only carry the gun between the time you sense the danger and the time the police or sheriff have arrived (put your gun away before the officers see you—you don't want them to think you're a threat and shoot you).

As discussed later in Chapter 6, you can't *use* a gun just to protect property, in spite of what this exception seems to say. If property is in danger, you can only have a gun in case you are attacked by the criminal, and not to protect the property.

Fear of Person Subject to Restraining Order

Exception to the Concealed Gun Law: Yes.

Exception to the Loaded Gun Law: Yes.

You may carry a concealed and/or loaded gun if you *reasonably* believe that you are in grave (very serious) danger from a person subject to a current, court-issued restraining order in which the court found that the restrained person poses a threat to your life or safety. If you are tried for violating the concealed gun law and/or the loaded gun law, the jury (or judge, if you do not have a jury trial) will decide whether a person in your situation would reasonably believe himself or herself to be in grave danger. This exception does not apply to mutual restraining orders issued under the Family Code unless the court has found that there is a specific threat to your life or safety.[12]

At Your Residence, Place of Business, or Private Property

Exception to the Concealed Gun Law: Yes.

Exception to the Loaded Gun Law: Yes.

Loaded Gun Law: You may have a loaded gun at your place of residence, including your temporary residence or campsite.[13]

45

The loaded gun law does not generally apply to residences, because you are not in a public place or on a public street while you are inside your house or apartment (you are *next* to a public street, but not *on* one). Therefore, you don't need an exception to the loaded gun law to have a loaded gun in a private residence. However, this exception is helpful for those times when your residence *is* a public place, such as when you are camping or staying in a motel.

If you are engaged in any lawful business, you may have a loaded gun in your place of business. Officers, employees, and agents *who are authorized by the business owner* may also have loaded guns (not concealed) while in the place of business. For this exception, "business" includes nonprofit organizations.[14]

If you own or lawfully possess (such as by a lease) any private property, you may have a loaded gun on that property.[15] Private property includes your garage and the area around your home that is part of your property.

Note that there's a difference between "have" and "carry." You can *have* a loaded gun in these places. But according to the courts, you can't *carry* the loaded gun around in a public place unless it's necessary to use it in a lawful way (such as for the Reasonable Belief of Immediate, Grave Danger exception, above).

Example

Appellate Court Case: People v. Overturf. Overturf was the owner and manager of an apartment complex. He hired a 20-year old to do gardening and other work in exchange for an apartment. Because the young man disturbed the other tenants with loud parties and excessive drinking, Overturf fired him. The young man came back to pick up his belongings with three of his friends. He demanded that Overturf pay him a certain amount of money, threatening to "knock his teeth down his throat" if he didn't pay. Overturf returned to his apartment and called the sheriff. He then saw the former tenant and his friends around his car, which was in the complex's driveway. Worried that they would damage the car, Overturf went to confront them, bringing his .22 pistol with him for protection. Overturf was 49 years old and suffered from severe rheumatoid arthritis. The other men were all between 19 and 21. When Overturf arrived in the driveway, he fired his .22 once into a pile of dirt. Because he took his loaded gun into the driveway, Overturf was tried and convicted of violating the loaded gun law.

Overturf appealed, arguing that the driveway was both his place of business and his private property, and that he therefore fell under an exception to the loaded gun law. The court painstakingly dissected the way the law was written, and stated that the while law allows a person to "have" a loaded gun, it says nothing about carrying it around. The court said it's okay to have a loaded gun in your residence, your place of business, or on your property, but you can't carry it around when your residence, business, or property is a public place unless it's "necessary to use it" in a lawful way. The court considered the Reasonable Belief of Immediate, Grave Danger exception as a legal way Overturf could have used his gun, and decided that Overturf's person and/or property were *not* in danger. The court ruled against Overturf.[16]

Comment: This was a surprising result based on the facts as stated in the court's decision—Overturf's person and property certainly seemed as if they were in danger. This case is proof that various judges and juries can view facts differently, and that legal results can be unpredictable.

Concealed Gun Law: You may carry a handgun concealed on your person or in your vehicle when you are in your residence, in your place of business, or on your private property. You must meet three conditions:[17]

1. You are over 18 years old;

2. You are a citizen of the United States or a legal resident; and

3. You are not in any class of people who are prohibited from having a gun, such as someone who has been convicted of a felony (see Chapter 1).

Only owners of businesses may carry concealed guns in their place of business. If you are an officer, employee, or agent, but not an owner, you can have a *loaded* gun in the place of business if you are authorized by the business owner. You can keep the gun behind the counter, or in another hidden place, without violating the concealed gun law. The concealed gun law applies only to guns hidden on your person or in your vehicle.

How do you know if you qualify as an "owner" of the business? You are an owner if you have a "proprietary, possessory, or substantial ownership" in the business.[18] What's "substantial" is not defined, but it would be safe to say that an interest of 50% or greater would meet the requirement. A "possessory" interest means you have the right to exclude other people from the workplace and the right to control activities at the workplace.[19] If you have either a substantial ownership interest or a possessory interest, you are an "owner" for the purposes of the concealed gun law.

A "place of business" must be a fixed location. A court in 1981 held that a taxi driver's taxi is a "place of business," and that the driver could carry a concealed, loaded gun in his cab, but that is no longer the law (except for taxi drivers).[20]

A more recent court decision stated that a place of business must be a fixed place, such as an office, store, or warehouse. In this case, a bounty hunter tried to convince the court that his pickup truck was his office. The court disagreed, and upheld his conviction for carrying a concealed gun in his truck. If a place of business did not have to be "fixed," the court said, salespeople, truck drivers, and others could all claim the place of business exception and have concealed and loaded guns in their vehicles.[21]

A residence must also be a fixed location. When someone lives in a van, for example, the van is not a residence while it is being driven on the public streets or highways, and the residence exception does not apply.[22]

Locked Container in Motor Vehicle

Exception to the Concealed Gun Law: Yes.

Exception to the Loaded Gun Law: No.

You may transport or carry an unloaded handgun, other concealable gun or flare gun in your car without violating the concealed gun law if you follow all of the following rules:[23]

1. You must be a U.S. citizen over the age of 18 years and you must not be in any class of people who are prohibited from having a gun, such as someone who has been convicted of a felony (see Chapter 1). (If you are not a U.S. citizen, you can transport your gun by using the exceptions listed in the next sections, starting on page 51.)

2. The gun must be inside a motor vehicle and must be locked in the vehicle's trunk or in a locked container *other* than the utility or glove compartment.

3. The gun must be carried by the person directly to or from the motor vehicle for any lawful purpose, *and, while carrying the gun, the gun must be in a locked container.*

4. A "locked container" means a secure container which is fully enclosed and locked by a padlock, key lock, combination lock, or similar locking device.

Comment: It has been suggested that a legal way to have a gun in a car would be to keep an unloaded gun in a locked bag on the seat of the car, with the key in the lock and a loaded clip in plain view on the seat next to the bag. This might allow relatively easy access to the gun in an emergency. This practice is *not* recommended because, while no published court decisions address this issue, a lock that is closed but that has a key in it would probably not be considered "locked" for the purposes of this exception.

The concealed gun law and the loaded gun law were intended to *prevent* citizens from having easy access to loaded guns in places where exceptions do not apply, especially while driving. Be aware that if you unlawfully brandish a gun at the driver of a motor vehicle, you are guilty of a felony (see page 164 for the laws on brandishing a gun).

Remember, this exception only authorizes you to carry a *concealed* handgun. Your gun can't be loaded or have ammunition attached to it unless you also fall under an exception to the loaded gun law.

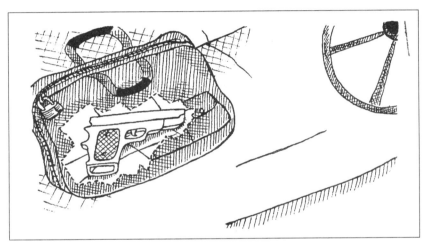

The handgun in this bag doesn't violate the concealed gun law even though it's in the passenger compartment of a car, because it's in a locked container, no ammunition is attached to the gun, and the gun owner carries it to and from the car in the locked bag (see text for detailed rules).

Belt Holsters

Exception to the Concealed Gun Law: Yes.

Exception to the Loaded Gun Law: No.

You can carry a handgun openly in a belt holster without violating the concealed gun law.[24] However, the gun can't be loaded or have ammunition attached to it while you are in a public place or on a public street, or you will violate the loaded gun law (the loaded gun law was passed in the first place because people were walking around with loaded guns on their hips). Additionally, unless you wear a uniform for a living you will probably attract a lot of unwanted attention even if your gun is not loaded!

Exceptions for Certain Situations

Additional exceptions exist that apply to specific situations where you can carry a concealed and/or loaded gun. Each of the exceptions states whether it is an exception to the concealed gun law, the loaded gun law, or both.

Two rules apply to all the exceptions listed in this section that are exceptions to the concealed gun law:[25]

1. You must go directly to, and come directly from, the event described in the exception with only reasonably necessary deviations (side trips); and

2. You must carry your gun *unloaded, in a locked container* other than a car's glove box or utility box. A "locked container" means a secure container which is fully enclosed and locked by a padlock, key lock, combination lock, or similar locking device. A car trunk is a locked container if it is locked and can't be reached from the passenger compartment without unlocking a lock.

Travel Between Residence, Place of Business, and Private Property

Exception to the Concealed Gun Law: Yes.

Exception to the Loaded Gun Law: No.

If you meet the requirements for the Residence/Place of Business/Private Property exception to the concealed gun law (page 45), you may transport a concealed gun while traveling directly between any of those places.[26]

Traveling to/from Campsite

Exception to the Concealed Gun Law: Yes.

Exception to the Loaded Gun Law: No.

If you are going directly to or coming directly from lawful camping activity where having a gun is not prohibited by state or local government agencies, you may transport a concealed gun so you can have the gun at the campsite for personal protection.[27] If you don't know whether you may have a gun at your campsite, contact the local law enforcement agency at the place you plan to camp.

Repair or Transfer of Gun

Exception to the Concealed Gun Law: Yes.

Exception to the Loaded Gun Law: No.

If you go to a fixed place of business or private residential property to have your gun lawfully repaired, or to lawfully transfer (sell, give, or lend) your gun, you may transport the gun concealed when you are going directly to or coming directly from this place.[28]

Taking Gun to Residence/Business/Property

Exception to the Concealed Gun Law: Yes.

Exception to the Loaded Gun Law: No.

If you meet the requirements for the Residence/Place of Business/Private Property exception to the concealed gun law (page 45), you may transport a concealed gun directly from the place where you lawfully took possession of the gun (such as a gun store) to your residence, place of business, or private property.[29]

Target Range Practice

Exception to the Concealed Gun Law: Yes.

Exception to the Loaded Gun Law: Yes.

If you are going directly to or coming directly from a target range that has a business or regulatory license (i.e., an established target range that is a business, not just a designated shooting area), you may transport a concealed, unloaded gun for the purpose of practicing with that gun at that range.[30]

You may have or carry a loaded gun while you are using any target range for the purpose of practicing shooting with the gun. In order to transport your gun to a range that does not have a business or regulatory license, follow the rules for the Locked Container in Motor Vehicle exception to the concealed gun law (page 49).[31]

Gun Club

Exception to the Concealed Gun Law: Yes.

Exception to the Loaded Gun Law: No.

If you are a member of any club or organization which is organized for the purpose of lawfully collecting and displaying guns, you may transport a concealed gun while you are at club meetings or while going directly to or coming directly from those meetings. The gun must be in a locked container "at all times."[32]

Safety/Sporting Event

Exception to the Concealed Gun Law: Yes.

Exception to the Loaded Gun Law: No.

You may transport a concealed gun when you are going directly to or coming directly from a recognized gun safety or hunter safety class, or a recognized sporting event involving the gun.[33]

Gun Show

Exception to the Concealed Gun Law: Yes.

Exception to the Loaded Gun Law: No.

You may transport your gun directly to and from a gun show or swap meet to which the public is invited, for the purpose of displaying the gun in a lawful manner. This includes going to or coming from gun shows or events sponsored by an organization devoted to the collection, competitive use, or other sporting use of guns, for the purpose of lawfully transferring (selling, giving, or lending) the gun.[34]

Concealed Carry License Issuance

Exception to the Concealed Gun Law: Yes.

Exception to the Loaded Gun Law: No.

You may transport a gun while going directly to or coming directly from a place designated by a sheriff or police chief, if you have been asked to go there so that the sheriff or police chief can decide whether to issue you a license to carry that gun concealed (CCW license).[35]

Persons Assisting Police by Request

Exception to the Concealed Gun Law: Yes.

Exception to the Loaded Gun Law: Yes.

If you have been summoned by any active or honorably retired peace (law enforcement) officer of California, or of any other state or the federal government, to assist the officer in making arrests or preserving the peace, you may have a concealed and/or loaded gun while you are *actually engaged* in assisting the officer.[36]

Citizen's Arrest

Exception to the Concealed Gun Law: No.

Exception to the Loaded Gun Law: Yes.

If you are making or attempting to make a lawful arrest, you may openly carry a loaded gun (not concealed).[37]

Gun Transfer at Police Station

Exception to the Concealed Gun Law: Yes.

Exception to the Loaded Gun Law: No.

You may transport a gun directly to or from a law enforcement agency so that you may transfer (sell, give, or lend) that gun to someone.[38]

Entertainment Production

Exception to the Concealed Gun Law: Yes.

Exception to the Loaded Gun Law: No.

If you are an authorized participant in a movie, TV, video production, or other entertainment event, you can have a concealed gun when you lawfully use the gun as part of the production or while going directly to or from the production. Also, if you are an authorized employee or agent of someone who supplies guns to be lawfully used in these productions, you can have a concealed gun when transporting the guns directly to or from a production. Note that this exception does not allow you to have a loaded gun.[39]

Transporting Gun for Family Transfer or after Receiving It by "Operation of Law"

Exception to the Concealed Gun Law: Yes.

Exception to the Loaded Gun Law: No.

If you transfer (sell, give, or lend) your gun to your parent, grandparent, child, or grandchild (see page 155), you may transport the gun to the place where you make the transfer.

55

The family member receiving the gun may transport it from that place. If you receive a gun by "operation of law," which includes as an executor or administrator of an estate, secured creditor, levying officer, receiver, bankruptcy trustee, and other methods, you may transport the gun in order to transfer it.[40]

Transporting Gun for DOJ Report or Buy-Back

Exception to the Concealed Gun Law: Yes.

Exception to the Loaded Gun Law: No.

If you obtain a handgun or transfer a handgun, and you wish to make an optional report of the transfer to the DOJ (see Chapter 9), you may transport the gun to a place to make the report. You may also transport the gun to an authorized gun buy-back program.[41]

Exceptions for Groups of People

The following people are exempt from the concealed gun law and/or the loaded gun law:[42]

Concealed Carry License Holders

Exception to the Concealed Gun Law: Yes.

Exception to the Loaded Gun Law: Yes.

If you have a license to carry a concealed gun (CCW license), you may carry a loaded handgun, either concealed or openly, depending on the nature of your license. See Chapter 4 for license requirements.[43]

Peace Officers

Exception to the Concealed Gun Law: Yes.

Exception to the Loaded Gun Law: Yes.

Most active and retired California peace (law enforcement) officers, peace officers from other states, and federal government agents while on official business can carry concealed and/or loaded guns. This exception also applies to certain retired federal agents. If you are an active or retired peace officer or federal agent, note that complex rules apply. You should look them up and read them carefully. The principal California Penal Code Sections are 12027, 12027.1, and 12031.[44]

Note: Patrol special officers appointed by the police commission, animal control officers and zookeepers, humane officers, and harbor police officers have separate rules for carrying loaded guns, including completing a regular course in firearms training. See Section 12031(c).

Gun Business

Exception to the Concealed Gun Law: Yes.

Exception to the Loaded Gun Law: No.

If you are in the business of manufacturing, importing, wholesaling, repairing, or dealing in guns, you may possess or transport concealed guns if you are licensed for that business, if the guns are merchandise, and if the guns are unloaded. This exception also applies to authorized employees and agents of people who meet these requirements.[45]

Military on Duty

Exception to the Concealed Gun Law: Yes.

Exception to the Loaded Gun Law: Yes.

You may carry a concealed gun if you are a member of the Army, Navy, Marines, or National Guard, when you are on duty. You may also carry a concealed gun if you are a member of an organization authorized by law to purchase or receive those guns from the military or National Guard.[46] Note: the wording of this law does not include the Air Force.

If you are a member of the military forces of California or of the United States, you may carry a loaded gun while in the performance of your duties.[47]

Military and Civil Organizations

Exception to the Concealed Gun Law: Yes.

Exception to the Loaded Gun Law: No.

Members of authorized military or civil organizations, while parading or when going to or from meetings of these organizations, may carry a concealed, unloaded gun.[48]

Employees of Common Carriers

Exception to the Concealed Gun Law: Yes.

Exception to the Loaded Gun Law: No.

Operators, employees, or agents of licensed common carriers (railroads, airlines, bus companies, etc.), may transport concealed, unloaded guns in conformance with federal laws that apply to transporting guns.[49]

Guards and Messengers

Exception to the Concealed Gun Law: Yes.

Exception to the Loaded Gun Law: No (See next section).

Guards or messengers of common carriers (railroads, airlines, bus companies, etc.), banks, and other financial institutions may have a concealed gun while actually employed in and about the transportation or delivery within California of any money, treasure, bullion, bonds, or any other thing of value.[50]

Dept. of Consumer Affairs Certificate Holders

Exception to the Concealed Gun Law: No.

Exception to the Loaded Gun Law: Yes.

The following groups of persons may carry a loaded gun *after* they have successfully completed approved courses in the carrying and use of guns and in the exercise of the powers of arrest, and after they have received a certificate from the Department of Consumer Affairs.[51]

Guards and Messengers: Guards or messengers of common carriers (railroads, airlines, bus companies, etc.), banks, and other financial institutions, while actually employed in and about the transportation or delivery within California of any money, treasure, bullion, bonds, or any other thing of value.[52]

Armored Vehicle Guards: Guards who are employed by armored contract carriers and who in the course of this employment carry deadly weapons,[53] and who are operating armored vehicles pursuant to California Highway Patrol and Public Utilities Commission authority, while acting within the course and scope of their employment. If a guard was hired before January 1, 1977, he or she does not have to complete the courses or receive a firearms qualification card from the Department of Consumer Affairs.[54]

Private Investigators: P.I.s, and their uniformed employees, who are licensed under the Private Investigator Act,[55] while acting within the course and scope of their employment.[56]

Private Patrol: Private patrol operators, and their uniformed employees, who are licensed under the Private Investigator Act,[57] while acting within the course and scope of their employment.[58]

Alarm Company Operators/Agents: Operators who are licensed under the Alarm Company Act,[59] while acting within the course and scope of their employment. Also uniformed alarm agents employed by an alarm company operator, while actually engaged in protecting and preserving the property of their employers, or while on duty, or while traveling to or from their residences, their job, or employer-required range training. (Note: cities and counties may have laws requiring alarm agents to register their names.)[60]

Uniformed Security Guards: Uniformed security guards who are regularly employed and paid as security guards by any lawful business, while actually engaged in protecting and preserving the property of their employers, or while on duty, or while traveling to or from their residences, their job, or employer-required range training.[61] Also uniformed security guards and night watch persons employed by any public agency, while acting within the course and scope of their employment.[62]

Members of Shooting Clubs

Exception to the Concealed Gun Law: Yes.

Exception to the Loaded Gun Law: Yes.

Members of any club or organization organized for the purpose of practicing shooting at targets on *established* target ranges, public or private, may carry concealed guns while the members are using the guns at the target ranges, or while going to or from the ranges. The guns must be unloaded during transportation to and from the range. This is similar to the Target Range Practice exception in the previous section, except that the two rules for transporting the gun do not apply.[63]

You may have or carry a loaded gun while you are using any target range for the purpose of practicing shooting with the gun. You may also have or carry a loaded gun if you are a member of a shooting club, while you are hunting on the premises of the club.[64]

Hunters/Fishermen

Exception to the Concealed Gun Law: Yes.

Exception to the Loaded Gun Law: No.

Licensed hunters or fishermen can carry a concealed gun while engaging in hunting or fishing, or while going to or coming from that hunting or fishing expedition.[65]

You don't need an exception to the loaded gun law when you lawfully hunt, because you are not in a "prohibited area" where it's illegal to shoot a gun, and therefore the loaded gun law doesn't apply. However, you cannot have a loaded gun in or on your vehicle while it's on any public road or highway, even when you're hunting.[66]

Signaling Flare Storage

Exception to the Concealed Gun Law: No.

Exception to the Loaded Gun Law: Yes.

A flare gun, rocket, or other emergency signaling device is considered a "gun" for the purposes of the concealed gun law and the loaded gun law. However, you can store these devices, loaded or unloaded, aboard any boat or airplane without violating the concealed gun law or the loaded gun law. You can also openly carry these devices (not concealed) while in a permitted hunting area or while going to or from a hunting area, if you are carrying a valid California permit or license to hunt with you.[67]

Picketing

Exception to the Concealed Gun Law: No.

Exception to the Loaded Gun Law: No.

The exceptions to the concealed gun law listed in this section do *not* authorize you to carry a concealed gun on your person or in your vehicle while picketing.

None of the exceptions to the loaded gun law authorizes you to carry a loaded gun on your person or in your vehicle while picketing.

Carrying a concealed or loaded gun while picketing is a misdemeanor. As used here, "picketing" includes any informational activities in a public place relating to a concerted (collective or united) refusal to work.[68]

Example: Putting Together a Set of Exceptions

Ex

Example

Here's how these exceptions might be combined in a normal, daily activity: You have a loaded handgun in your desk drawer at your business. You can keep a gun this way because you own the business or because you're an employee authorized to have a loaded gun by the business owner. This is the Residence/Place of Business/Private Property exception to the loaded gun law.

When you leave for home at the end of the day, you remove the ammunition from the gun, and put the gun in a locked briefcase. You leave the ammunition at the office or carry it in your pocket. If you're carrying a clip, you must either carry it openly, so it's not concealed, or without ammunition in the locked case. You carry the gun to your car in the locked briefcase. This is how you have to carry a gun when you're carrying it concealed on your person and you're taking advantage of the Locked Container in Motor Vehicle exception and most of the other exceptions to the concealed gun law. Remember, a gun in your purse, briefcase, knapsack, etc., is considered a gun on your "person," when you're carrying the bag around.

You put the locked briefcase in your car. You drive to your home, and carry your gun into your home in the locked briefcase. This is the Travel Between Residence/Place of Business/ Private Property exception to the concealed gun law.

When you are in your home, you once again load the gun and keep it under the Residence/Place of Business/Private Property exception to the concealed gun law and the loaded gun law (making sure any children can't get to it, of course).

It sounds complicated, but it's really not. Just break it up into each place where you want to have a gun and try to find an exception that matches that place. You can have a gun in those places where an exception applies to you.

Summary: Transporting Your Gun in Your Vehicle

Rifles and shotguns are not covered by the concealed gun law. However, they are covered by the loaded gun law. You can have your rifle or shotgun anywhere in your vehicle, concealed or not. It can be in the passenger compartment, the trunk, or anywhere else (see page 72 for how you must transport the gun when you are in a school zone). But it can't be loaded or have ammunition attached to it in a position where it is ready for firing, unless you fall under an exception to the loaded gun law.

Handguns (and other "concealable" guns and flare guns) are covered by both the concealed gun law and the loaded gun law. You can transport one in your vehicle by following the rules for the "Locked Container in Motor Vehicle" exception to the concealed gun law (see page 49).

The best way to transport your handgun is to unload it, put it in a a fully-enclosed, secure case or bag, and lock the case or bag with a small padlock, key lock, or combination lock. Ammunition cannot be attached to the gun in a position where it is ready for firing. When the gun is in this case, you can transport it in your car and you can carry it to and from any of the places where an exception to the concealed gun law applies to you. When you transport the gun in your car in this manner, you can put it any place in your car except for the glove box or the utility box.

Penalties for Violating the Concealed Gun Law and the Loaded Gun Law

If you are caught with a concealed, loaded gun in violation of the concealed gun law and the loaded gun law, you can be charged with two crimes. It is common for defendants with a clean record to be charged with misdemeanor violations of both the concealed gun law and the loaded gun law. A plea bargain is often offered where the defendant pleads guilty to one misdemeanor, and the other charge is dropped.

Any conviction for a crime in the Firearms chapter of the Penal Code (Sections 12000-12101), however, can have serious future implications for your gun rights. Once you have a conviction for violating the concealed gun law, the loaded gun law, or any other Firearms chapter law, if you carry illegally again and are caught you risk being convicted of a felony. As a felon, you would lose your right to have a gun of any kind. This is in addition to a possible prison term!

Here are the penalties for violations of the concealed gun law and the loaded gun law:

Violation is Felony

The violation of either law is a felony if any of the following apply to you:[69]

1. You have previously been convicted of any felony, *or of a violation of any of the laws in the "Firearms" chapter of the Penal Code* (Sections 12000-12101).

2. The concealed and/or loaded gun is stolen, and you know or have cause to believe it is stolen.

3. You are an active participant in a criminal street gang.

4. You are in a class of persons who is prohibited from having a gun under California law.

5. You are not in lawful possession of the concealed and/or loaded gun. "Lawful possession" means you either own the gun, or have permission to posses it. This permission can come from of the owner, or from a person who apparently has the authority to possess it. If you take a gun without permission, however, you do not have lawful possession of it.

Violation is Felony/Misdemeanor

If you do not fall into one of the above felony categories, the violation of either law is a felony/misdemeanor if you have previously been convicted of a crime against a person or property that was not a felony, or of a narcotics or dangerous drugs violation that was not a felony.[70]

Crimes against a person include assault, battery, sexual assault, and more. Crimes against property include burglary, forgery, theft, embezzlement, false personation, insurance crimes, business crimes, and more.

Violation is Misdemeanor

If you do not fall into one of the above felony categories or the above felony/misdemeanor category, the violation of either law is a misdemeanor.[71] This misdemeanor is punishable by imprisonment in the county jail of not more than one year, and/or by a fine of not more than $1,000.

Minimum 3-Month Sentence for Previous Violators

If you are convicted of violating either law and the court imposes a punishment of probation or a suspended sentence, you must still serve at least three months in the county jail if you have previously been convicted of a violation of any of the laws in the "Firearms" chapter of the Penal Code (Sections 12000-12101), or if you have previously been convicted of a misdemeanor involving the violent use of a gun listed in Section 12001.6 (see page 13).[72]

You must also serve a minimum of three months if you are convicted of violating the concealed gun law and you have a previous conviction for any felony (this applies to the concealed gun law only, and not to the loaded gun law).

In unusual cases where the interests of justice would best be served by imposing a lesser sentence than the minimum three months, however, the court can impose a lesser sentence.[73]

There are two minor differences between the penalties for the concealed gun law and the loaded gun law:

Under the loaded gun law, if you have previously been convicted of a felony that is not part of the Firearms chapter of the Penal Code, there is no three-month minimum sentence.

Also, if you violate the loaded gun law and receive one year or less in the county jail, the law provides that it will not count as a conviction of a crime punishable by imprisonment for a term of more than one year for the purposes of determining whether you can have a gun under federal law. The concealed gun law does not have a similar provision.[74]

Remember: If you unlawfully carry a gun that is both concealed and loaded, you are violating two different laws. Even though the penalty for the violation of each law is basically the same, you can be charged, convicted, and sentenced for two separate crimes.

Endnotes

1. Penal Code § 12001(a), (d).
2. People v. Smith (1946) 72 Cal.App.2d Supp. 875, 879.
3. People v. Hale (1974) 43 Cal.App.3d 353, 356.
4. 38 Cal.Ops.Atty.Gen. 199 (1961).
5. Penal Code § 12001(d).
6. Penal Code § 12031(g); People v. Clark (1996) 45 Cal.App.4th 1147, 1154.
7. People v. Dillard (1984) 154 Cal.App.2d 261, 266.
8. People v. Vega (1971) 18 Cal.App.3d 954, 958.
9. Penal Code § 12031(f).
10. Penal Code § 12031(e); People v. Kern (1979) Cal.App.3d 779, 782; People v. Zonver 132 Cal.App.3d Supp. 4.
11. Penal Code § 12031(j)(1).
12. Penal Code §§ 12025.5, 12031(j)(2).

13. Penal Code § 12031(l).
14. Penal Code § 12031(h).
15. Penal Code § 12031(h).
16. People v. Overturf (1976) 64 Cal.App.3d Supp. 1, 6-7.
17. Penal Code § 12026.
18. Stats. 1989, ch. 958, § 2 (8 Cal. Legis. Serv. (West) 2988-2989).
19. People v. Barela (1991) 234 Cal.App.3d Supp. 15, 20.
20. People v. Marotta (1981) 128 Cal.App.3d Supp. 1, 7.
21. People v. Wooten (1985) 168 Cal.App.3d 168, 175.
22. People v. Melton (1988) 206 Cal.App.3d 580, 590.
23. Penal Code § 12026.1.
24. Penal Code § 12025(e).
25. Penal Code § 12026.2(b).
26. Penal Code § 12026.2(a)(4).
27. Penal Code § 12626.2(a)(12).
28. Penal Code § 12026.2(a)(5).
29. Penal Code § 12026.2(a)(6).
30. Penal Code § 12026.2(a)(9).
31. Penal Code § 12031(b)(5).
32. Penal Code § 12026.2(a)(2).
33. Penal Code § 12026.2(a)(3).
34. Penal Code §§ 12026.2(a)(7), (15); 27 CFR 178.100(b).
35. Penal Code § 12026.2(a)(10).
36. Penal Code §§ 12027(a), 12031(b)(1).
37. Penal Code § 12031(k).
38. Penal Code § 12026.2(a)(11).
39. Penal Code § 12026.2(a)(1), (a)(8).
40. Penal Code § 12026.2(a)(13).
41. Penal Code § 12026.2(a)(14), (a)(16).
42. Penal Code § 12027.
43. Penal Code §§ 12027(j), 12031(b)(6).
44. Penal Code §§ 12027(a), (i), 12031(b).
45. Penal Code § 12027(b).
46. Penal Code § 12027(c).
47. Penal Code § 12031(b)(4).
48. Penal Code § 12027(d).
49. Penal Code § 12027(h).

50. Penal Code § 12027(e).
51. Penal Code § 12031(d).
52. Penal Code § 12031(d)(1).
53. *See* Bus. & Prof. Code § 7521.
54. Penal Code § 12031(d)(2).
55. Bus. & Prof. Code Ch. 11.5, Section 7512, et seq.
56. Penal Code § 12031(d)(3), (d)(6).
57. Bus. & Prof. Code Ch. 11.5, Section 7512, et seq.
58. Penal Code § 12031(d)(3), (d)(6).
59. Bus. & Prof. Code Ch. 11.6, Section 7590, et seq.
60. Penal Code § 12031(d)(3), (d)(5).
61. Penal Code § 12031(d)(5).
62. Penal Code § 12031(d)(4).
63. Penal Code § 12027(f).
64. Penal Code § 12031(b)(5).
65. Penal Code § 12027(g).
66. *See* § 374c; Fish & Game Code §§ 2006, 3002.
67. Penal Code § 12031.1.
68. Penal Code § 12590.
69. Penal Code §§ 12025(b)(1)-(b)(4), 12031(a)(2)(A)-(a)(2)(D).
70. Penal Code §§ 12025(b)(5), 12031(a)(2)(E).
71. Penal Code §§ 12025(b)(6), 12031(a)(2)(F).
72. Penal Code § 12025(c)(1), (c)(2), 12031(a)(5)(A).
73. Penal Code §§ 12025(d), 12031(a)(5)(B).
74. Penal Code § 12031(a)(6).

Chapter 3: What Places Have "Extra" Restrictions on Guns?

Certain places in California have laws restricting guns that are separate from the concealed gun law and the loaded gun law. In these places, the penalties for carrying a gun can be more severe than for the concealed and loaded gun laws, and the exceptions to those laws do not apply. The concealed gun law and the loaded gun law are still enforced in these places. The laws in this chapter are "extra" gun restrictions.

Public Government Buildings and Meetings

You can't possess a gun, loaded or not, in any state or local public government building or at any public government meeting.[1] This law also applies to certain knives with blades over 4 inches, and to other weapons. Violation is a felony/misdemeanor. After a misdemeanor conviction for this offense, you can't have a gun for 10 years.[2]

A state or local public government building is any building of which the government owns or leases at least part, and where government employees regularly go to perform their official duties. It includes courthouses, but it does not include places where government employees live. A public government meeting is any meeting of any level of the state or local government that's required to be open to the public.

This law does *not* apply to:

❏ Persons who bring weapons into a court so those weapons can be used as evidence (unless the person is a party to an action in that court). This exception does not apply to federal courts.

❏ Persons who have a license to carry a gun (CCW license).

❏ Certain active and retired peace officers,[3] and persons summoned by such a peace officer to assist the officer in making arrests or preserving the peace, while those persons are actually assisting the officer.

❏ Persons with written permission to have a specific gun, given by the authorized official in charge of security for the government building. Also, certain on-duty, licensed security guards[4] hired by the owner or manager of the building, if they have the same written permission.

❏ Persons who lawfully live in, possess, or own the building, when they are in the portions of the building that are not owned or leased by the government.

State Capitol/Legislative Residences

You can't have a loaded gun in any of the following places:[5]

❏ The California State Capitol building and its grounds, bounded by 10th, L, 15th, and N Streets in Sacramento.

❏ Any legislative office.

❏ Any office of the Governor or of any other consti-tutional officer. A constitutional officer is some-one who holds a position created by the California Constitution, such as Members of the Senate or Assembly, Secretary of State, Controller, etc.[6]

❏ Any hearing room where a Senate or Assembly committee is conducting a hearing.

❏ The building and grounds of the following: the Governor's mansion, any other residence of the Governor, the residence of any other constitu-tional officer, or the residence of any Member of the Legislature.

This law does *not* apply to:

❏ Persons who have a license to carry a gun (CCW).

❏ Certain peace officers,[7] and persons summoned by such a peace officer to assist the officer in mak-ing arrests or preserving the peace, while those persons are actually assisting the officer.

❏ Members of the United States or Calif. military forces engaged in the performance of their duties.

❏ The Governor, other constitutional officers, Members of the Legislature, members of their immediate families, and people acting with their permission, with respect to their own residences.

Violation is a felony/misdemeanor. After a misdemeanor conviction for this offense, you can't have a gun for 10 years.[8] A gun is "loaded" for the purpose of this particular law when one person has both the gun and ammunition that can be fired from the gun in his or her possession. Police officers can examine any gun on the grounds of a place cov-ered by this law to determine whether the gun is loaded.[9]

Schools and Colleges

Both California and federal law have created a special type of area with gun restrictions—a "school zone." It is illegal to possess any gun in a place that you know, or reasonably should know, is within a school zone. A school zone is any place in, on the grounds of, or within 1,000 feet of the grounds of any public or private school that teaches any of grades kindergarten through 12.[10]

Violation of the California school zone law is a felony punishable by two, three, or five years in the state prison (under certain circumstances, violation is a misdemeanor). If you recklessly fire or attempt to fire a gun in a school zone, you are guilty of a felony punishable by three, five, or seven years. It is a misdemeanor to have any ammunition or ammunition-related devices (such as a clip) on school grounds.[11]

The penalty for violation of the federal law is up to five years in prison, up to a $5,000 fine, or both. If no prison time is given, a federal violation is considered a misdemeanor.

California law also prohibits the possession of any gun on the grounds of any public or private university or college campus. The "grounds" include all college and university property, *including residence halls.* Violation is a felony, punishable by one, two, or three years in the state prison. If the gun is loaded, the penalty is increased to two, three, or four years. A gun is "loaded" for this law in exactly the same ways it's loaded for the loaded gun law (see page 39).

A similar law prohibits you from having a taser, stun gun, air gun, and most knives in a school, college, or university. See Section 626.10 for details.

Exceptions

The following are exceptions that allow you to have a gun in a school zone and/or on the grounds of a college or university. Each exception states the areas to which it applies:

You can't have a gun, loaded or not, within 1,000 feet of the grounds of any public or private school. See text for exceptions.

❑ Residences, businesses, and private property that are not part of school grounds, as long as you possess the gun(s) in those places legally. (K-12, College/University)

❑ Handguns that are unloaded, and in a locked container or in the locked trunk of a motor vehicle. A locked container means a secure container which is fully enclosed and locked by a padlock, key lock, combination lock, or similar locking device. (K-12)

❑ Rifles, shotguns, and other guns that are not capable of being concealed on the person, while they are being lawfully transported in a motor vehicle. In a K-12 school zone, they must be in a locked container or in a locked gun rack on a motor vehicle. (K-12, College/University)

❑ Persons who have a license to carry a concealed gun (CCW license). (K-12, College/University)

❑ Persons who have written permission from: the school district superintendent or the equivalent school authority, when the person is using the gun in an approved school program (for K-12 schools); the university or college president or the equivalent university or college authority (for colleges and universities), or a person designated by one of these people. (K-12, College/University).

❑ Certain peace officers[12] (K-12, College/University), and persons summoned to assist such officers in making arrests or preserving the peace, while those persons are actually assisting the officers (College/University only).

❑ Security guards and retired peace officers who are authorized to carry a loaded gun under Section 12031. For K-12 school zones, the guards must have a gun license issued by the state. This exception does not allow these persons to possess ammunition or ammunition feeding devices on the grounds of a K-12 school. (K-12, College/University)

❑ Armored vehicle guards[13] engaged in the performance of their duties. An armored vehicle guard is a person employed by an armored contract carrier who in the course of such employment carries a deadly weapon. (K-12 if licensed to carry a gun by the state; College/University)

❑ Members of the United States or California military forces engaged in the performance of their duties (College/University).

Because both California and federal law apply to K-12 school zones, and because you must follow whichever law is stricter, only exceptions that work for both laws are listed.

Note that some of the exceptions to the concealed gun law and/or the loaded gun law that allow you to carry a gun on the street, such as the Reasonable Belief of Immediate, Grave Danger exception and the Fear of Person Subject to a Restraining Order exception, *do not work* in school zones and in colleges and universities.

Playgrounds and Youth Centers

If you violate any of the following laws while you are on a playground, or while you are in a youth center when it is open for operation, and you know that you are on a playground or in a youth center, you are guilty of a felony/misdemeanor:[14]

❑ Carrying a concealed handgun on your person or in your vehicle (the concealed gun law)—Section 12025.

❑ Carrying a loaded gun on a public street or in a public place (the loaded gun law)—Section 12031.

❑ Drawing or brandishing a gun in a "rude, angry, or threatening manner" in the presence of another person, or using a gun in a fight or quarrel, except in self defense—Sections 417(a)(2) and 417(b).

A "playground" is any park or recreational area designed to be used by children that has play equipment installed. It includes sports fields, basketball courts, and similar facilities located in public or private schools or public parks.

A "youth center" is any public or private facility used to host recreational or social activities for minors, when minors are present. A youth center is open for operation when it is open for business, classes, or school-related programs, or at any time when minors are using the facility.

The felony/misdemeanor punishment for this crime is in addition to any punishment you receive for the "underlying" crime of unlawfully carrying or brandishing a gun.

Polling Places

You can't have a gun at a polling place (a place where people go to vote in government elections), or in the immediate vicinity of a polling place. Violation is a felony, including imprisonment or a fine of $10,000, or both.[15]

This law does *not* apply to:

❑ Persons who have written authorization to have a gun at the polling place from the appropriate city or county elections official.

❑ Certain private guards and peace officers.[16]

This law *does* apply to persons who have a license to carry a gun (CCW license).

Federal Buildings and Courthouses

Fed
Federal Law

If you bring a gun or attempt to bring a gun into a federal building or other facility (other than a courthouse), you can be fined and/or imprisoned for up to one year.[17] If you have a gun in the facility and intend to use it in a crime, you can be fined and imprisoned for up to five years. Federal facilities include post offices and other places run by the federal government.

This law does *not* apply to:

- ❑ Law enforcement officers performing official duties.

- ❑ Federal officials or armed forces members authorized by law to have a gun in a federal facility.

- ❑ People lawfully carrying guns in a federal facility incident to hunting or other "lawful purposes."

  While carrying a gun is generally lawful for people with a license to carry a gun (CCW license), it is unclear whether this is the type of "lawful purpose" contemplated by this law. CCW license holders—carry guns in federal facilities at your own risk!

If you bring a gun or attempt to bring a gun into a federal *court* facility, you can be fined and/or imprisoned for up to two years.[18]

This law does *not* apply to:

- ❑ Law enforcement officers performing official duties.

- ❑ Federal officials or armed forces members authorized by law to have a gun in a federal facility.

Note that the "lawful purposes" exception does *not* apply for court facilities. California CCW licenses don't allow you to carry a gun in a federal court facility.

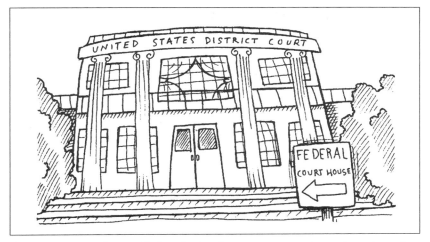

Carrying a gun into a federal courthouse can send you to prison for two years, even if you have a license to carry a gun.

Airports and Airplanes

If you bring any gun into a "sterile area" of an airport terminal or onto a commercial aircraft, or you place a loaded gun in your checked baggage, or you attempt to do so, you are guilty of a federal offense punishable by a fine of up to $25,000 and up to five years in a federal penitentiary. A "sterile area" is any area where access is controlled by security personnel, such as the boarding gates. A gun is loaded when there is ammunition in the chamber, cylinder, clip, or magazine.[19]

You may transport *unloaded* guns or ammunition on airplanes by placing them in your checked baggage and informing the airline that you are transporting guns. Call the airline in advance for detailed rules.

Other Places

This chapter does not cover every place in California where guns are restricted. For example, many California counties prohibit guns in county parks. County and city laws are separate from the state's concealed and loaded gun laws, and the exceptions to those state laws do not apply. If you have a gun in a county park in a county which prohibits guns in parks, you could be charged with a crime even if it would be legal for you to have a gun outside of the park.

It's up to you to investigate your local county and city laws, and the laws at campgrounds and on federal lands. You can find county and city laws at your main library branch or in the law library of your county courthouse. The books are called County or Municipal Codes or Ordinances (such as "Los Angeles County Code"). Look in the index under "firearms," "guns," "ammunition," "weapons," and any other topic that could apply to guns, then look up the code sections. Call the ranger or the local law enforcement agency before you camp. Keep in mind that laws change, so stay up to date.

Endnotes

1. Penal Code §§ 171b, 18.
2. Penal Code § 12021(c)(1).
3. *See* Penal Code § 171b(b)(2).
4. *See* Penal Code § 171b(b)(7).
5. Penal Code §§ 171c, 171d.
6. *See* Government Code § 75030.5.
7. *See* Penal Code §§ 171c, 171d.
8. Penal Code § 12021(c)(1).
9. Penal Code § 171e.
10. Penal Code § 626.9; 18 USC §§ 921(a)(25), 922(q), 924(a)(4).
11. Penal Code § 12316(c).
12. *See* Penal Code § 626.9(c).
13. *See* Bus. & Prof. Code § 7581(e).
14. Penal Code § 626.95.
15. Elections Code § 29634.
16. *See* Elections Code § 29634(b).
17. 18 U.S.C. § 930(a).
18. 18 U.S.C. § 930(b).
19. 49 U.S.C. App. § 1472(l); 14 C.F.R. § 107.21.

Chapter 4: How Can You Get a Permit to Carry a Gun?

What Is a License to Carry a Concealed Weapon?

You do not need a license or permit to have loaded or unloaded guns in your home, or in any other place where the concealed gun law, the loaded gun law, and other gun laws don't restrict your right to have a gun (see Chapter 2 and Chapter 3). If you want to carry a loaded gun in your vehicle, on the street, in public places, or in other places where guns are restricted, and you do not fall under an exception listed in Chapter 2 or Chapter 3, you must have a permit that allows you to do so.

A license to carry a concealed weapon is a permit that allows you to carry a handgun. The license is commonly called a "CCW" license, for "carry concealed weapons." A CCW license lets you carry a gun anywhere in the state of California, with the exception of certain federal property such as courthouses.

Depending on where you live in California, it can be easy or extremely difficult to obtain a CCW license. Whether you will be issued a license is completely within the discretion of the sheriff of your county and the police chiefs of the departments in your county. They alone decide who gets a license and who doesn't. If you live in a rural county, you may have a good chance of obtaining a license, depending on your sheriff. If you live in the City of Los Angeles, you stand little chance of receiving a license from the LAPD or L.A. County Sheriff, unless you are an unusual applicant such as a jeweler who regularly carries large amounts of gems or cash. The LAPD and L.A. County Sheriff issue very few licenses.

Frequently, sheriffs and police chiefs add their own restrictions to getting a license. Many police chiefs issue licenses only to residents of their cities. Sheriffs and police chiefs also sometimes require that an applicant post a bond, buy an insurance policy, take an expensive gun training course, and/or live in the county or city for a certain number of years before they will issue the applicant a license.

The decision on whether you will be issued a license to carry a concealed gun is made by your county sheriff or police chiefs.

California citizens don't have any legal "right" to be issued a CCW license, even if they meet the requirements.[1] Various lawsuits have been filed, and continue to be filed, to force law enforcement agencies to adopt uniform standards for who will get a permit, but at this time no uniform standards exist. The decision is up to your local sheriff and police chiefs.

Detailed Rules for Getting a License (Section 12050)

Where to Apply: Licenses are issued by the county sheriff and by the chief or head of any municipal (city) police department in your county. The law allows you to request a license from any municipal chief of police or from the county sheriff, but many police chiefs will only issue a license to someone who lives or works in their city.

Applicant Must Prove: To get a license, you must prove that you:

1. Are of good moral character;

2. Have good cause to be issued a license; and

3. Are a resident of the county where the license will be issued.

These things are "proved" by completing the application and by having your Department of Justice (DOJ) background check come back clean. There are no set standards for what constitutes "good cause." What is good cause to one sheriff or police chief may not be good cause to another. You just have to make the best case you can for why you need a license.

No License if Prohibited Class: You can't be issued a license if the DOJ determines that you are in a class of persons who are prohibited from having a gun. If you have already been issued a license, that license will be revoked if the DOJ notifies the issuing law enforcement agency that you are prohibited from having a gun.

Details of License: The license is a permit to carry a pistol, revolver, or other firearm capable of being concealed upon the person. It does not authorize you to carry rifles or shotguns. Licenses are issued in two formats:

1. A license to carry a concealed gun (which also exempts you from the loaded gun law).

2. A license to carry a loaded and exposed gun. This "open carry" format is available only in counties with a population of less than 200,000 persons as measured by the most recent federal 10-year census, and only lets the license holder carry a gun inside that county.

Term: The license is valid for up to one year from the date its issued. Reserve or auxiliary peace officers appointed according to Section 830.6 may have licenses valid for up to three years.

Restrictions on License: A license may include any reasonable restrictions that the sheriff or police chief decides are warranted. These include restrictions on the time, place, manner, and circumstances under which the license holder may carry the gun. Any restrictions must be stated on the license.

If there are no restrictions, a concealed-carry license holder may carry the gun anywhere in the state of California. Federal law takes precedence over California law, however, and CCW licenses may not be valid for certain federal facilities and lands such as courthouses. See Chapter 3 for places with "extra" gun restrictions.

Change of Address: If you have a CCW license and you change your place of residence, you must notify the law enforcement agency that issued the license within 10 days after you move.

A license to carry a concealed gun cannot be revoked just because the license holder moves to another county, unless there is some other reason for revoking the license. A license to carry a loaded and exposed gun *must be revoked* immediately if the license holder moves to another county.

Application for a License (Section 12051)

The application for a license must be in writing and be signed by the applicant. It must be on a standard form used statewide, and must include the following information:

1. Name.

2. Occupation.

3. Residence and business addresses.

4. Age, height, weight, hair color, and eye color.

5. The reason for wanting to carry a gun.

6. The answers to eight questions, such as whether you have ever been denied a CCW license and whether you have been committed to a mental institution, that will help the sheriff or police chief determine whether or not to grant you a license.

7. A statement by the applicant that all the information on the application is true.

If a license is issued, most of the above information will be stated on the license. The license will also have a description of the gun or guns the license holder can carry, including the name of the manufacturer, the serial number, and the caliber. New in 1995, the license may be laminated.

The applicant must give a set of his or her fingerprints. The fingerprints will be sent to the DOJ, where they will be checked along with other records to determine whether the applicant is prohibited from having a gun.[2]

The applicant must pay a modest application fee based on the DOJ's costs for checking the applicant's fingerprints and records, along with an additional fee of up to $3 to cover the costs of the sheriff or police department for processing the application.[3] Many sheriff and police departments charge a substantially higher annual license fee once a license has been issued, however.

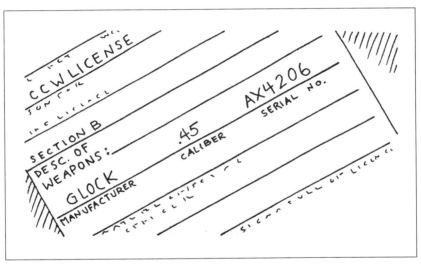

A concealed weapons license lists the gun(s) you can carry on the face of the license. The license holder can only carry the guns listed.

If an applicant has previously applied for a license from the same sheriff or police department, and that department sent the applicant's fingerprints to the DOJ, no new fingerprints or application form are required. If an applicant has previously been issued a license by a different sheriff or police department, and that department sent the applicant's fingerprints to the DOJ, no new fingerprints are required.[4]

84

Amending (Changing) a License

If you have a license and you want to change the terms of the license, you can apply to the law enforcement agency that issued you the license for the license to be amended.[5]

An application for an amendment requires that you fill out a standardized form, but does not require a new fee or fingerprints. You must sign the application, and must state the type of change desired and the reason for the change.

If the license is amended, you will be issued a new license, but the expiration date of your original license won't be extended. Possible amendments are:

❑ Adding or deleting the authority to carry a particular handgun.

❑ Authorization to carry a concealed handgun, if the original license was to carry a loaded and exposed handgun.

❑ Authorization to carry a loaded and exposed handgun (in counties of 200,000 persons or less).

❑ Changes in any conditions or restrictions on the license.

Penalty for Lying on an Application

If you lie on the application for a license or an amendment about having a previous CCW license denied or revoked, a criminal conviction, a finding of not guilty by reason of insanity, the use of a controlled substance (drugs), a dishonorable discharge from military service, a commitment to a mental institution, or a renunciation (giving up) of United States citizenship, you are guilty of a felony. If you lie about any other statement on the application, you are guilty of a misdemeanor.

Endnotes

1. Nichols v. County of Santa Clara (1990) 223 Cal.App.3d 1236, 1239.

2. Penal Code § 12052.

3. Penal Code § 12054.

4. Penal Code § 12052(b), (c).

5. Penal Code § 12050(f).

6. Penal Code § 12051(c).

Chapter 5: When Can You Shoot Someone in Self-Defense?

What Is Homicide?

Homicide is when one person kills another. The term is neutral—it describes the act of killing, but does not pass moral or legal judgment. A homicide is not necessarily a crime.

To learn when you can shoot someone in self-defense, it helps to know the basic classes of homicide: criminal, excusable, and justifiable. Criminal homicides include murder and manslaughter. Excusable homicides include accidental killings in which no one was careless, and accidental killings during certain sudden fights. Justifiable homicides include intentional but legally blameless acts such as one person shooting another in self-defense, and the state executing a condemned prisoner. There are no punishments for excusable and justifiable homicides.[1]

What Is Murder? Murder is the unlawful killing of a person with malice (malice is technically called "malice aforethought"). There are four situations in which the court can find the defendant acted with malice:[2]

1. Defendant had an intent to kill or to cause serious bodily injury.

2. Defendant killed without being sufficiently provoked.

3. Defendant acted with an "abandoned and malignant heart," which means a total disregard for human life. (Example: Shooting a gun into a crowd of people even though you don't intend to hit someone.)

4. Defendant killed someone during the commission of a dangerous felony.

Murder is punishable by various terms in the state prison (beginning with "15 years to life"), and by death, depending on the degree and situation.

What Is Manslaughter? Manslaughter is the unlawful killing of a person without malice. There are two kinds of manslaughter (not including vehicular manslaughter, which is killing while driving a motor vehicle or boat):[3]

❑ **Voluntary:** Defendant had an intent to kill, but no malice. This happens if the killing is in a sudden quarrel or heat of passion, or in an honest but unreasonable belief in the need to use deadly force to defend oneself (i.e., *when mistaken about the right to use deadly force in self-defense*).[4] Punishable by imprisonment in the state prison for three, six, or eleven years.

❑ **Involuntary:** Defendant had no intent to kill and no malice. This happens when someone kills during the commission of a misdemeanor which is inherently dangerous to human life, or when someone does a dangerous but lawful act while being careless and accidentally kills someone. Punishable by imprisonment in the state prison for two, three, or four years.

When Is Homicide Justifiable?

According to the justifiable homicide statute (law), you may use deadly force in the following situations.[5] However, *you must follow the basic rule of self-defense*, which is discussed in the next section, or you may not have a legal right to self-defense and you could be convicted of manslaughter or murder.

❑ You can protect yourself or anyone else from being murdered or seriously injured by a criminal.

❑ You can prevent a violent felony from being committed.

❑ You can defend your habitation (the place where you live), your property, and your person against violent felonies, and against any person who is trying to force his or her way into your habitation so that he or she can use violence against a person inside.

❑ You can apprehend (capture) a violent felon with deadly force if necessary, or lawfully suppress any riot, or keep and preserve the peace. *(Note: This is a **very** limited right. See below.)*

The Basic Rule of Self-Defense

Most of the laws that let you use deadly force in self-defense were written a long time ago, and are rambling and unclear. Over the years, the courts have interpreted these laws, and court opinions are now an important part of the law of self-defense. The basic rule of self-defense is a combination of different rules the courts have added to the law.

89

You should read the basic rule carefully, as well as the other rules that follow. The rules are explained in detail after each one is stated. Several examples are included, which will help you remember the rules.

The Basic Rule of Self-Defense Is:[6]

In order to use deadly force to defend yourself, you must have an **honest and reasonable belief** that you are in **imminent danger** of death or **great bodily injury** from an **unlawful attack,** and that your acts are **necessary** to prevent the injury.

Here is an explanation of each of the parts of the rule:

Belief Must Be Both Honest and Reasonable

In order to use deadly force when you're faced with a threat from another person, you must actually and honestly believe four things:

1. You are at risk of losing your life or of suffering great bodily injury from an attack.

2. The attack is unlawful.

3. There is an imminent danger of this attack.

4. The action you take to defend yourself is necessary to prevent your death or injury.

And, if a "reasonable person" were standing in your shoes, the situation would have to cause the same beliefs in that person and that person would have to have taken the same action.

What Is "Reasonable?"

"Reasonable" is what the average prudent (practical and wise) person in your situation would do. What is "reasonable" is decided by the jury (that's one reason why a jury is composed of different members of the community—it helps determine what is "reasonable" behavior). If you are charged with a crime after using a gun in self-defense, the jury will determine whether your beliefs and actions were reasonable.

Unfortunately, there is no way to know in advance what kind of behavior a particular jury will find "reasonable." The identical case could be tried before two different juries with two different results. One jury might want to reward the defendant for his or her actions, while another will convict him or her. Clearly, there are some predictable results. It would be unreasonable to shoot someone for holding you up with what is obviously a banana. But when you're closer to the edge of the law, the result can be unpredictable.

What if You Were Not "Reasonable"?

If you honestly believed you were in danger of being killed or seriously injured, but your belief was unreasonable, you can be convicted of voluntary manslaughter if you kill your attacker, and of assault and/or battery if you attack but don't kill him or her.[7] The same is true if you unreasonably believed that the attack was imminent, or was unlawful, or that it was necessary to respond to the attack with deadly force.

Ex
Example

Let's say you were terrified of spiders. You have heard that some spiders can kill people, but you don't know exactly what they look like. Someone approaches you with a small brown spider in his hand, and he threatens to drop it on you. Believing it is a deadly spider, you pull out a gun and shoot him. It turns out it was only a common garden spider. Even though you were honestly afraid for your life, would a reasonable person have been so afraid of the spider? This is for a jury to decide. If a jury didn't believe that a reasonable person would have feared death or great bodily injury, you could be convicted of voluntary manslaughter if your shot killed him.

Even though you may fear for your life, you can't shoot unless a "reasonable person" would also have the same fear.

Prior Threats Count for What Is "Reasonable"

If your attacker has made earlier threats against you, the jury may consider this when deciding whether your beliefs and actions were reasonable. Remember, however, that before you shoot there still must be an imminent threat (one that is about to happen). Also, just because a jury *considers* prior threats, it doesn't mean your actions were reasonable.

> **Ex**
> **Example**

Appellate Court Case: People v. Pena. Pena was friends with Ambrosio. Ambrosio was a violent person, and Pena once saw him savagely beat two young girls. Ambrosio had bragged to Pena about committing armed robberies and vicious assaults. Ambrosio was also a martial arts expert and was known in the community as a violent person. Pena was 5' 7" and 160 pounds; Ambrosio was 6' 1" and 241 pounds. Pena hired some employees who had previously worked for Ambrosio, and Ambrosio became angry. He said that Pena had "stabbed him in the back." Ambrosio started making threats against Pena. He called Pena and told him, "Be sure to look behind every time you turn around." Pena stayed home for three days, then started carrying a .44 magnum revolver wherever he went. His employees begged him not to carry the gun, but he refused to give it up. He was genuinely afraid for his life. Pena was with his friends at a bar when Ambrosio walked in the door. Smiling, he walked up to Pena. Pena drew his gun and fired one shot, killing Ambrosio. He was charged with murder, and the jury found him guilty of voluntary manslaughter. The trial court had refused to instruct the jury that it could consider the effect of Ambrosio's prior threats against Pena when it evaluated the shooting.

Pena appealed, arguing that the jury should have considered the whole history of his relationship with Ambrosio, not just what happened the night of the shooting at the bar. The Court of Appeal agreed and ordered a new trial for Pena. It said that the jury must consider prior threats of death or great bodily harm made by the deceased (dead person) against the defendant when considering whether the defendant acted as a reasonable person would act in protecting his or her own life or bodily safety.[8]

You Can Act on How Things Appear to You

Whether you were "reasonable" will be judged by the situation as it *appeared* to you, not how it actually was. You can act in an honest and reasonable belief in your imminent danger. You will not be held criminally accountable later if things turn out to be not as they seemed, as long as your beliefs and actions were both honest and reasonable.[9] Remember, however, that a jury decides what is reasonable, and results of jury trials can be unpredictable.

Danger Must Be Imminent

To justify using deadly force, the danger to your life or safety, as you see it, must be imminent (about to happen). An imminent danger is one that you must deal with instantly.

Ex
Example

Appellate Court Case: People v. Aris. Aris's husband beat her regularly and severely during their ten-year relationship. One night he told her that he didn't think he'd let her live until morning. He then fell asleep in the bedroom. She testified that she believed he was serious, and that she was afraid of what would happen when he woke up. Aris got a handgun from the kitchen and shot her husband five times in the back as he slept. A jury convicted her of second degree murder, with a sentence enhancement for using a gun. She was sentenced to a prison term of 15 years to life.

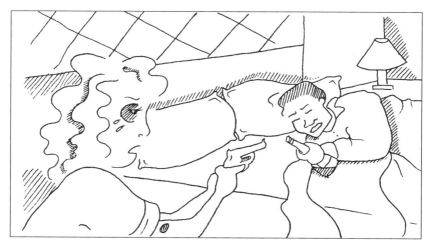

In this situation, the woman has no right to shoot because there is no imminent threat.

Aris appealed the case. The Court of Appeal said: "[T]he danger that justifies homicide must be imminent and a mere fear the danger will become imminent is not enough." No jury composed of reasonable persons could conclude that a sleeping person presents an imminent danger of great bodily harm, the court stated. The court also pointed out that Aris could have left the house to escape [note that this seems to contradict the well-established principle that you don't have to retreat]. The court did say that Aris was entitled to have an expert witness testify on battered woman syndrome, and that the jury could use this to decide whether Aris had an honest but unreasonable belief in the danger (which would reduce the killing from murder to voluntary manslaughter). However, the court upheld Aris's conviction of murder.[10]

Comment: Aris *would* have been justified in shooting her husband *as* he was beating her or if he was *about* to beat her, only if the beating threatened her life or would likely cause her great bodily injury. Some believe this was a harsh decision—the court could have ordered that the case be retried so the jury could decide whether Aris, as a battered woman, honestly believed she had no other choice and no means of escape (which would result in a conviction of voluntary manslaughter).

Home Protection Rule—Presumption of Reasonable Beliefs

The California Legislature has enacted a law that helps people in their homes defend themselves from intruders while lessening the fear of legal consequences. This law gives the resident the benefit of the doubt and establishes a presumption that the very act of forced entry is a threat to the life and limb of the homeowner or apartment dweller.

When you are in your residence and you shoot an intruder, you are *presumed* to have a reasonable fear of imminent danger of death or great bodily injury if three elements are present:[11]

1. An **intruder unlawfully and forcibly enters your residence**, or has unlawfully and forcibly entered your residence.

2. The intruder is **someone who is not a member of the family** or the household.

3. **You know** or have reason to believe **that an unlawful and forcible entry has occurred**.

You come home and find that a back window has been broken and opened, and that your silverware drawers have been ransacked. You have reason to believe that an unlawful and forcible entry occurred.

If the above three elements are true, you are presumed to have a reasonable fear of imminent danger of death or great bodily injury to yourself, your family, or a household member when you shoot at the intruder. When you have a reasonable fear of imminent death or great bodily injury, you are entitled to use deadly force in self-defense, thus your use of deadly force is presumed to be reasonable as well.

In this situation, you are presumed to be reasonable if you use deadly force in self-defense (see text for important details).

The effect of the home defense presumption is that the district attorney has the burden of proving beyond a reasonable doubt that you did *not* have reasonable fear when you pulled the trigger. (Remember, you must also have had an actual, honest fear.)

If you don't meet the requirements for this presumption because, for example, there was no forced entry or the attacker was a household member, this doesn't mean that you can't prove self-defense. It just means you can't take advantage of the *presumption* of reasonable fear. You must show enough evidence in court that you had a reasonable fear of imminent danger of death or great bodily injury from an unlawful attack to convince the jury that you acted in proper self-defense.[12]

Ex
Example

Appellate Court Case: People v. Brown. Brown hired Neal to lay some bricks for a flower bed at his house. It appeared to Brown that Neal was going to be late in finishing the job, and Brown fired him. Neal became angry and started knocking bricks off the flower bed wall with a hammer. Brown yelled at him to stop. Brown says that Neal then walked up to his front porch with the hammer raised in his hand. The porch was on a walkway open to the street. There was no gate or other barrier between the porch and the street. There was only a screen door between Neal and Brown, and Brown believed his safety was at risk. He shot Neal in the leg with a pistol while Neal was on the porch. This ended the argument. Brown was charged with assault with a deadly weapon and with the use of a gun in committing the crime (which would increase his sentence). The jury was given the standard instruction on self-defense, but was not given the instruction for the home defense presumption. The jury convicted Brown.

Brown appealed, arguing that he should have been allowed the home defense presumption. The Court of Appeal refused Brown's argument. It said that you can only have the home protection presumption where you have a reasonable expectation of safety (such as inside your residence). Brown had no reasonable expectation of safety on his front porch. Anyone could have walked up to the porch without breaking any social rules, the court said—Girl Scouts selling cookies, the newspaper carrier, door-to-door salespeople, and so on. Therefore, the element of *forcible and unlawful entry* failed, because an entry onto Brown's front porch was not an entry into his residence. The entry onto a front porch that has no barriers to the street is not an entry into your residence.[13]

Danger Must Be Unlawful

The danger you're threatened with must be unlawful, such as a robbery or an assault. The "danger" of being lawfully arrested by the police or of someone entering land or property he or she has a right to enter does not justify your using deadly force in self-defense.[14]

Reasonable Force

When defending yourself, you can use only the force necessary to repel the attack. Any force which exceeds that amount is not justified. If you use excessive force, you expose yourself to criminal charges and civil lawsuits.

If an attack is deadly or is likely to cause great bodily injury, then you can respond with deadly force or force likely to cause great bodily injury. But you must put up with a misdemeanor assault, such as a punch from someone who is not physically overwhelming or a trained fighter, without the privilege of retaliating with deadly force or force likely to cause the puncher great bodily injury (you *can* defend yourself with a level of lesser force that is sufficient to prevent the puncher from injuring you).[15]

Example

Appellate Court Case: People v. Clark. Clark had a two-year extramarital affair with Gayle, a woman he met at work. When Clark's wife found out about the affair, she threatened to tell Gayle's husband. To "head her off at the pass," Gayle told her husband and terminated the affair. Gayle's husband refused to drop the matter, however. He made numerous verbal threats against Clark, attempted to confront Clark, and engaged Clark in two truck chases. Clark began carrying a loaded gun in his truck. The conflict reached a peak when the husband used his truck to block Clark's way into his driveway. The man got out and approached Clark in his truck, saying, "Your time is now." As he reached into Clark's truck, Clark shot him in the chest. Although Clark gave the man first aid, he died. Clark was found guilty of involuntary manslaughter, and was granted probation instead of prison. He was also ordered to make payments to the man's four minor children.

Clark appealed his conviction, arguing that he acted in legitimate self-defense. The Court of Appeal rejected Clark's argument. It said that, while there was no question Clark had the right to defend himself from the attack, there was no evidence that the man wanted anything other than a fist fight. The man was not so physically overwhelming that Clark had reason to fear great bodily injury from a fist fight, the court said.[16]

Other Self-Defense Rules

Pursuing and Punishing the Attacker

Right Ends after Attack Ends: If you defend yourself so successfully that the attacker is no longer capable of injuring you, you have no right to continue to fight in self-defense. You cannot further injure or kill the attacker for punishment or revenge.

Not only can't you punish the attacker, you can't even have a *desire* to punish the attacker when you make the decision to use deadly force to defend yourself! You can have only fear. It's acceptable to feel anger and other emotions at the time. But if a desire to punish the attacker is a factor in your *decision* to use deadly force, it can "poison" your legitimate right to self-defense.[17]

Appellate Court Case: People v. Shade. Shade was at his friend's house. Cress kicked in the front door, pointed a .22 caliber rifle at Shade, and said, "I'm going to kill you." Shade and Cress fought, and Shade knocked Cress unconscious. Shade and his friend left the house. When they came back later, Shade beat the still-unconscious Cress to death with Cress's gun. Shade was convicted of murder and sentenced to life in prison. Shade argued on appeal that the jury should not have been instructed that the person who kills must act on fear alone, saying that it should be okay to act on fear combined with other emotions. The court disagreed. You can't have a desire to harm your attacker, even if it is combined with fear, the court said.[18]

Pursuit of Fleeing Attacker: There is a *very limited* right to pursue the attacker. If the fleeing attacker still represents a real and reasonable threat of serious injury, you may pursue him or her until you have made yourself safe from the danger. This right can only be used to protect the victim of the attack, not to punish an attacker attempting to escape.[19]

Be careful with this right—if the attack has ended, and there is no more danger, do not shoot or pursue the attacker!

You have no right to shoot after the attack has ended.

No Retreat Requirement

In General: If you are attacked, you don't have to retreat, no matter where you are. You may stand your ground and defend yourself, if necessary, with deadly force.[20]

Exception—Can't Start Fight: If you wrongfully attack someone, or if you voluntarily participate in a fight, you lose the right to use force in self-defense. Because you have lost the right of self-defense, you no longer have the right to stand your ground and defend yourself.

In order to regain your right of self-defense, you must in good faith try to withdraw from the fight or quit your attack, and you must communicate your intent to your opponent. Once you attempt to withdraw *and inform your opponent* that you have quit the fight or attack, you have a new right to stand your ground and defend yourself from any new and further attack, using deadly force if necessary.[21]

If your opponent has had a chance to quit the fight, and he or she continues to fight, this is considered a new assault by the opponent.

Note: You have no right to use force in self-defense if you start a fight or argument just so you can force (or trick) your opponent into a deadly confrontation and thus create a real or apparent need for your own attack.[22]

Original Attack Not a Felony: If your attacker does not attempt an attack likely to cause serious bodily injury or death, but only commits a simple assault or a trespass, you have no right to use deadly force in defense. If you respond with deadly force, the *attacker* has a right to self-defense. The attacker must *still attempt to withdraw* before defending himself or herself, but if your counter-attack is so sudden and dangerous that the attacker has no chance to withdraw, the attacker may resort to self-defense immediately.[23]

Example

Appellate Court Case: People v. Gleghorn. Fairall was angry with Downes because she sold Fairall's stereo without his permission. He smashed all the windows of Downes' car, slashed her tires, dented the body, kicked in her locked door, scattered her belongings, and broke an aquarium, freeing her snake. Downes told her friend Gleghorn about what Fairall did. Gleghorn went to the garage Fairall called home, and pounded on the door, saying Fairall should come out so Gleghorn could kill him. When Fairall didn't come out, Gleghorn opened the door, and found Fairall sleeping on a bed in the rafters. Gleghorn beat on the rafters with a stick, and set fire to some of Fairall's clothes, saying he would burn him out. Fairall kept a bow and arrow next to his bed, and he fired an arrow at Gleghorn which hit Gleghorn in the back. Gleghorn then beat Fairall to a pulp, causing very serious injuries. Gleghorn was convicted of simple assault and of battery with the infliction of serious bodily injury (a felony/misdemeanor).

Gleghorn appealed, arguing that he was entitled to use deadly force to defend himself after Fairall launched the arrow attack. His rationale was that he had committed only a simple assault by beating on the rafters with a stick and starting the fire, and that when Fairall launched the potentially-deadly arrow attack he had a right to use deadly force in self-defense. The court rejected this argument on two grounds. First, the court said, Fairall acted reasonably in shooting the arrow, because it *appeared* that his life was in danger. He had no way of knowing of any "secret intent" of Gleghorn to commit only a simple assault. Second, Gleghorn continued to beat Fairall long after Fairall was disabled and no longer posed any threat. The court upheld Gleghorn's conviction.[24]

Preventing Crimes and Capturing Criminals

You may use deadly force to prevent only some crimes and to capture only some criminals. You may use deadly force, only when necessary, to stop people from committing these crimes:[25]

- ❑ A felony involving a danger of great bodily harm.

- ❑ Dangerous conduct that may not be a felony, if you use force to "lawfully" suppress a riot, or to "lawfully" keep and preserve the peace.

- ❑ You may also use deadly force, when necessary, to arrest a person who has committed a felony involving a danger of great bodily harm.

This book does not discuss in what situations you can "lawfully" suppress a riot or keep and preserve the peace. You should assume that, even though these laws are on the books, the situation will almost *never arise* in which you can do so lawfully. This book also does not provide a list of crimes that are felonies, although the following are examples of four felonies that involve a danger of great bodily harm: murder, mayhem (mutilating somebody), rape, and armed robbery.

Warning—Don't Take the Law into Your Own Hands: Even though it is technically allowed by law, if you are not a peace officer you should not attempt to enforce the law. Public officers are not personally liable for a mistake in enforcing the law. A private citizen has no such immunity. If you make a mistake and falsely arrest someone, especially using a gun, or shoot someone in an attempt to arrest them or to stop a riot or keep the peace when you have no legal right to, you will probably be sent to jail, or be sued and lose, or both. This does not mean you should not defend yourself or your loved ones—you should, by all means necessary. But leave catching criminals to the police.

If you are not a police officer, you should not attempt to stop a riot—you could be sued and/or end up in jail. You are limited to protecting your life and the lives of others.

Ex
Example

Appellate Court Case: People v. Piorkowski. Piorkowski was walking to a liquor store to buy some cigars. As he passed a dry cleaning establishment, he noticed three youths steal a wallet from behind the counter. He told the dry cleaning manger to call the police, then chased after the youths. Piorkowski pulled a pistol he was carrying, and ordered the youths to halt. Two complied, but one continued to run. Piorkowski caught him, and they fought. During the fight, Piorkowski fired his gun into the youth's head, killing him. He immediately said, "My God, it was an accident." Piorkowski was charged with murder, and the jury convicted him of involuntary manslaughter. He was sentenced to 180 days in jail plus 3 1/2 years probation.

Piorkowski appealed the case, arguing that a person may justifiably commit a homicide when apprehending a person who has committed a felony. The Court of Appeal rejected Piorkowski's appeal, saying that deadly force may be directed toward the arrest of a felony only where the felony committed is one which threatens death or great bodily harm (a "forcible and atrocious" crime). There was no justification for Piorkowski's shooting the youth, the court said, because the youth did not commit a crime that threatened death or great bodily harm. Even his brandishing the gun to order the youths to halt was negligent and excessive, the court said.[26]

Ex
Example

Appellate Court Case: People v. Walton. Walton believed that the new occupants of a house down the block were dealing drugs. He called the police five or six times, but it did no good. One day he was working outside his house when he saw two men parked in a car. He believed they had come to buy drugs at the house down the block. He told them to get away from his house or he would "put holes" in their car. They left. Walton went inside his house and got a pistol which he put in a holster. Twenty minutes later, two other men parked down the street. Believing they were also there to buy drugs, Walton walked up to the driver, pulled his pistol from the holster, and pointed it through the open car window. The driver also had a gun. He and Walton engaged in a full blown shoot-out, during which Walton was shot in the abdomen. As it turned out, the occupants of both cars were undercover police officers who had come to arrest the residents of the house down the street for drug dealing. Walton was convicted of assault with a deadly weapon, with sentence enhancements for using a gun and for brandishing a gun. His sentence was six months in the county jail and two and one-half years probation.

Walton appealed, arguing that he was justified in using "self-help" measures to enforce the law because the police had failed to keep his neighborhood safe. The court rejected this argument, saying our legal system does not permit such self-help measures. The court also said that, while Walton did not make a citizen's arrest, a citizen who tries to make one can use no more force than reasonably necessary.[27]

No Crime if Missed Shot Hits Bystander

If you are properly acting in self-defense, but your shot misses and you injure or kill an innocent person, you are not guilty of a crime. Your intent to shoot your attacker was legal, and this intent is "transferred" to the innocent bystander.[28] Note, however, that you most likely will be sued by the innocent victim or his or her family.

Prohibited Person Can Use Gun in Emergencies

A person who is in a group of people who are prohibited from having a gun (see Chapter 1) has a limited right to use a gun in self-defense.

Example

Appellate Court Case: People v. King. King was in a class of persons who are prohibited from having a gun. He was at his friend's birthday party when some uninvited guests started causing trouble. They started a fight with other guests on the apartment's balcony. Soon eight friends of the trouble makers showed up. The host announced that the party was over and most guests and the trouble makers left. The uninvited guests tried to force their way back into the apartment, and more fighting broke out. Most of the remaining guests sought refuge in the bedroom and called the police. The troublemakers were trying to break down the door. King did not participate in any of the fighting. He was sitting at a table in the dining room when one of the uninvited guests threw a double hibachi grill through the adjacent window. King was hit with the hibachi and showered with glass, some of which got in his eyes. A guest in a wheelchair was also hit by glass. King and the other guest sought refuge in the bedroom, while the uninvited guests kept trying to break in. Some of the female guests were screaming and crying for someone to "do something." A woman guest handed King her .25 caliber Beretta pistol which she kept in her purse. The police still had not arrived and King was scared. He fired three shots into the air, which stopped the fighting. Then one intruder said King's gun had blanks in it, and the intruders rushed King. King fired another shot over their heads, and they retreated. Unbelievably, King was charged with two counts of assault with a deadly weapon and with a violation of Section 12021, which makes it a felony for certain prohibited people to possess a gun. He was found not guilty of ADW, but was found guilty of violating Section 12021. The court granted him probation instead of jail, but he appealed because he did not believe he should have a felony conviction on his record.

The California Supreme Court reversed the conviction. It said that prohibited people have a right to defend themselves and others in the same situations as non-prohibited people, and may use a gun according to the following rules:[29]

1. They didn't have a "preconceived design" or plan to get the gun;

2. The gun is made available to them by someone else;

3. They possess the gun only for the period where it is necessary to use the gun for defense;

4. They use the gun only if there is no other option. If they are defending themselves (as opposed to others), they must retreat if possible (unlike non-prohibited people);

5. They cannot have substantially contributed to the emergency situation; and

6. They cannot create a greater danger by obtaining and using a gun than the danger they are trying to avoid.

Under federal law, the same rules apply with one additional condition: people prohibited by federal law from having a gun must not recklessly place themselves in a situation where they need to use a gun in self-defense.[30]

No Punishment for Justifiable Homicides or Assaults

As stated earlier, if a homicide is justifiable there is no criminal punishment. If there is a trial and the defendant is found to have been justified, the defendant must be fully acquitted and discharged.[31]

There is also no criminal punishment for assault if you lawfully shoot in an attempt to defend yourself and miss, or if you end the attack just by showing your gun. There is no punishment for battery if you lawfully shoot your attacker but do not kill him or her. The crimes of assault and battery both punish *unlawful* attacks; if you follow all the self-defense rules, your use of force to defend yourself will not be unlawful.[32]

A justifiable homicide is a "privileged act." This means that a dead criminal's family can't sue you in civil court and win money if you kill a criminal in lawful self-defense.[33] (An injured criminal probably has no legal right to win money, either, but courts have not yet considered this issue.)

For important additional information on the legal reality of using deadly force in self-defense, see page 162.

Endnotes

1. *See* Penal Code §§ 195-197, 199.

2. Penal Code §§ 187, 188, 190.

3. Penal Code §§ 192-193.5.

4. In re Christian S. (1994) 94 D.A.R. 6607; People v. Flannel (1979) 25 Cal.3d 668; *see also* CALJIC 8.40.

5. Penal Code § 197; *see also* Penal Code §§ 692-694, Civ. Code § 50.

6. *See, e.g.,* People v. Aris (1989) 215 Cal.App.3d 1178, 1186.

7. In re Christian S. (1994) 94 D.A.R. 6607; People v. Flannel (1979) 25 Cal.3d 668.

8. People v. Pena (1984) 141 Cal.App.3d 462, 476.

9. People v. Clark (1982) 130 Cal.App.3d 371, 377; *see also* People v. Dawson (1948) 88 Cal.App.2d 85, 96, People v. Torres (1949) 94 Cal.App.2d 146, 151.

10. People v. Aris (1989) 215 Cal.App.3d 1178, 1188, 1192.

11. Penal Code § 198.5; *See, e.g.,* People v. Owen (1991) 226 Cal.App.3d 996.

12. People v. Gleghorn (1987) 193 Cal.App.3d 196, 203.

13. People v. Brown (1992) 6 Cal.App.4th 1489, 1495.

14. 2 Witkin & Epstein, *California Criminal Law 2d,* § 239(a)(3).

15. People v. Clark (1982) 130 Cal.App.3d 371, 380; CALJIC 5.30; Penal Code §§ 692, 693.

16. *Id.* at 380-381.

17. Penal Code § 198; People v. Trevino (1988) 200 Cal.App.3d 874.

18. People v. Shade (1986) 185 Cal.App.3d 711, 716.

19. CALJIC 5.50; Witkin & Epstein, at § 246(2).

20. People v. Clark (1982) 130 Cal.App.3d 371, 377; *see generally* Witkin & Epstein, at § 244.

21. Penal Code § 197(3); CALJIC 5.54; Witkin & Epstein, at § 245.

22. CALJIC 5.55; People v. Garnier (1950) 95 Cal.App.2d 489, 496 (dicta)(Woman started argument with man, then shot him.).

23. People v. Gleghorn (1987) 193 Cal.App.3d 196, 201; *see also* Witkin & Epstein, at § 245(c).

24. People v. Gleghorn (1987) 193 Cal.App.3d 196, 203.

25. Penal Code § 197(1), (4).

26. People v. Piorkowski (1974) 41 Cal.App.3d 324, 330.

27. People v. Walton (1982) 136 Cal.App.3d 76, 79.

28. People v. Matthews (1979) 91 Cal.App.3d 1018, 1024.

29. Rules 1-4: People v. King (1978) 22 Cal.3d 12, 24; Rules 5-6: People v. Pepper (1996) 41 Cal.App.4th 1029, 1035.

30. U.S. v Sahakian (9th cir. 1992) 965 F.2d 740; U.S. v. Lemon (9th cir. 1987) 824 F.2d 763, 765.

31. Penal Code § 199.

32. Penal Code §§ 240, 242, 692-694.

33. Gilmore v. Superior Court (1991) 230 Cal.App.3d 416, 420.

Chapter 6: When Can You Shoot Someone in Defense of Other People or Property?

Overview

Before reading this chapter, you should read Chapter 5, "When Can You Shoot Someone in Self-Defense?" You need to know the basic legal principles discussed in that chapter.

You may use deadly force to defend other people in the same manner as you may defend yourself. You may not use deadly force to protect property, except when the safety of people is at stake. You may, however, use limited force to eject trespassers from your property.

Defending Other People

California law lets you protect the lives or safety of others in exactly the same manner as you may protect yourself. The rule is the same as the Basic Rule of Self-Defense (discussed in detail in Chapter 5), with some simple changes:

In order to use deadly force to defend another person, you must have an **honest and reasonable belief** that the **other person** is in **imminent danger** of death or **great bodily injury** from an **unlawful attack,** and that your acts are **necessary** to prevent the other person's injury.[1]

Remember to follow all the self-defense rules discussed in Chapter 5.

Defending Property

There are two kinds of property, "real" and "personal." You should know the difference between them, both for reading this book and for understanding the law in general.

"Real" property means land and things that are considered permanently attached to land. Real property includes your house, the apartment building you live in, your trailer home, the land under those structures, and things attached to the land such as trees or crops.

"Personal" property refers to all other possessions, such as your money, car, furniture, art, and animals.

No Deadly Force to Protect Personal Property

As much as you may want to, you can't use deadly force or force likely to cause great bodily injury just to protect personal property. The law values human lives, even the lives of criminals, far more than any possession. Because the use of a gun is deadly force, you can't use a gun just to protect personal property.

Several laws seem to allow you to use deadly force to protect "property." These include Penal Code Sections 197 and 693, and Civil Code Section 50. But California courts have interpreted these sections to restrict them to situations where people are in danger.[2]

Homicide or the use of deadly force is justified only if the crime which is being defended against is a "forcible and atrocious" crime (i.e., an atrocious (bad) crime committed by force). Forcible and atrocious crimes are crimes that create a fear of death or great bodily harm.

Examples of forcible and atrocious crimes include murder, mayhem (mutilating somebody), rape, and robbery. Burglary may or may not be a forcible and atrocious crime, depending on the circumstances. If there are no people in the house, then there is no danger to human life or safety, and it's not a forcible and atrocious crime. If there are people in the house, the intrusion may create a legitimate fear for their safety, depending on the circumstances.[3]

You can't use deadly force or force likely to cause great bodily injury to protect property.

Ex
Example

It is late at night. You hear a noise in the carport and go to investigate, bringing your gun with you. You find a thief breaking into your car. You can't use your gun to stop the thief, because theft from an unoccupied auto is not a forcible and atrocious crime. You can't use your gun to stop the thief from fleeing (running away), because you are not under attack. But if the thief attacks you and threatens you with death or great bodily injury, you are entitled to use your gun to defend yourself, if you follow all the legal requirements for self-defense.

Comment: Legally, you are better off if you do *not* go outside your residence to investigate a burglar. If neither you nor any other household members are in immediate danger, your actions may be seen later by the police or the burglar's attorney as provoking a possibly deadly confrontation. This could result in your being prosecuted for a crime or sued by the injured burglar (or the dead burglar's family) if the burglar attacks you and you shoot him or her. The law in this area is not clear. You have to balance your desire to protect your property against possible legal consequences. It's legal to carry a gun on your own property for your protection (see Chapter 2 for certain limitations). But the legally safest way is this: If there is no danger to people, don't go outside. Call the police instead.

Note: Don't walk around outside with a gun if the police are on their way! Don't go looking for the burglar; you have a big advantage over an intruder if you stay put and let the intruder come to you. Stay in one room with other household members, and don't let the police see you with a gun—you don't want a police officer to think you're the burglar and shoot you.

"Protecting" Real Property

As with personal property, deadly force cannot be used simply to protect real property. But in the case of real property, peoples' lives may be at stake. If people are in danger of death or great bodily harm, you may use force of any kind, up to deadly force, when necessary, to protect people (while following all the rules of self-defense, of course).

An example of such a situation would be if a criminal were attempting to set fire to your house with you inside. If you shot the arsonist, you wouldn't be using deadly force to protect your property; you'd be protecting the safety of people inside.

Limited Right to Use Force to Eject Trespasser from Real Property

The law allows you to use force in order to eject a trespasser from your property when it would appear to a reasonable person that the trespasser will damage your property or injure household members or guests. First, you must ask the trespasser to leave the property, and give the trespasser a reasonable time to go. Then, you may use only the amount of force which is reasonably necessary to eject the trespasser.[4]

Example

Note that the "reasonable person" standard applies here three times. Here's an example of how it works. Let's say your front lawn is your prized possession. You have spent many hours trimming and fertilizing it, and every time you look at it you beam with pride. A strange family decides to have a picnic right in the middle of your lawn. They are crushing the grass and dripping ketchup and mustard on it. Believing your property is being damaged, you shout, "Get off my lawn!," wait five seconds, then eject the trespassers by running them over with your riding mower.

Your actions probably wouldn't pass the "reasonable person" tests. First, was your property *really in danger* of being damaged? The average prudent (wise) person would have to think so for you to have the right to eject the trespassers. Second, did you give the trespassers *enough time to comply* with your request to leave? If your lawn is huge, and the trespassers were in the middle of it, five seconds might not be a reasonable time. Third, did you use *only the force necessary* to eject the trespassers? Even if you had a right to eject these grass-crushers, if the average prudent person would think of an effective but less forceful method, such as pushing the trespassers off the lawn, your using the mower was excessive force. Remember, a jury decides what's reasonable.

113

In order to use force to eject a trespasser, you must be the lawful owner or occupant (such as a renter) of residential property. Residential property is property where somebody lives. If any person who has a right to be on the property has invited the trespasser to be on the property, the invited person will probably not be considered a "trespasser," and you can't eject them.

When you are ejecting the trespasser, if the trespasser responds with force you are entitled to resist force with force, increasing it as the trespasser resists. But you can't use deadly force or force likely to cause great bodily injury just to eject the trespasser, unless the trespasser uses that same level of force against you, a household member, or a guest.

Can You Set an Automatic Trap with Your Gun?

No. This is called a "boobytrap." Some people want to use a gun or other device to protect property when they are not there, such as a vacation cabin, or to automatically protect their home when they are inside. They set up a gun to fire in the direction of the door or window when an unauthorized person trips a wire.

The legal definition of a "boobytrap" is: "Any concealed or camouflaged device designed to cause great bodily injury when triggered by an action of any unsuspecting person coming across the device." Types of boobytraps include guns, ammunition, or explosive devices attached to trip wires or other triggering mechanisms, sharpened stakes, and lines or wire with hooks attached.[5]

This is an example of a "boobytrap." Setting a boobytrap is a felony.

Any person who assembles, maintains, or places (or causes to be placed) a boobytrap is guilty of a felony, punishable by two, three, or four years in the state prison. Possession of a boobytrap with the intent to use it is a felony/misdemeanor, including imprisonment and/or a fine of $5,000. Possession and use of boobytraps may also be punished by the laws that cover bombs and other "destructive devices." Additionally, if your boobytrap *works*, you can be charged with murder.[6]

Comment: Not only is it illegal to set a boobytrap, any person whose boobytrap injures someone will almost certainly be sued and lose. A boobytrap cannot discriminate between right and wrong. Police officers, fire fighters, and children are among its potential victims. Even a burglar who is injured by one will probably win in a civil suit, because a burglar poses no threat to anyone's life or safety when no one is there, and this makes any use of force unjustified.

Endnotes

1. CALJIC 5.32; Penal Code §§ 197(1), (3), 692, 693, 694; Civ. Code § 50.
2. People v. Ceballos (1974) 12 Cal.3d 470, 482-483.
3. People v. Ceballos (1974) 12 Cal.3d 470, 478-479.
4. People v. Miller (1946) 72 Cal.App.2d 602, 606; CALJIC 5.40.
5. Penal Code § 12355(c).
6. Penal Code § 12355(a),(b).

Chapter 7: What Guns and Ammunition Are Illegal?

It is a felony/misdemeanor to possess, manufacture, or sell (or to import into California, offer for sale, give, or lend) any of the guns, gun devices, or ammunition listed below, unless an exception applies.[1]

In order to be convicted, you don't need to *know* your gun, gun device, or ammunition is illegal.[2] You just need to know you *have it* in your possession. It is up to you to investigate your guns, gun devices, and ammunition to ensure they comply with the law!

Illegal Guns

Short-Barreled Shotguns and Short-Barreled Rifles: A short-barreled shotgun (sometimes called a "sawed-off" shotgun) is any gun that fires a fixed shotgun shell and has a barrel length of less than 18" or an overall length of less than 26". A short-barreled rifle is any rifle with a barrel length of less than 16" or an overall length of less than 26".[3]

Federal law also regulates short-barreled shotguns and rifles. Any person transporting these guns in interstate commerce can be fined and imprisoned for up to five years.[4]

The overall length of a shotgun or rifle is measured by a single *straight* line, parallel to the bore, from the front of the barrel to the back of the stock. If the shotgun or rifle has a folding stock, the gun must be measured with the stock *closed*. There is no California law on how barrel length is measured, but federal law may offer some guidance. Under federal law, the barrel length of a rifle or shotgun is the distance between the muzzle and the face of the bolt, breech, or breachlock when closed and when the shotgun or rifle is cocked.[5]

Courts have been very harsh with people who were caught in possession of a short-barreled gun but who said they didn't know it was illegal, and with people whose guns were even a fraction of an inch under the minimum. In 1989, the Court of Appeal upheld the conviction of a woman who was storing a short-barreled shotgun that had belonged to her deceased brother. In response to her statement that she had no idea it was an illegal gun, the court said that you don't have to know the gun you have is illegal, you just have to know that it's a gun and that you have it in your possession. The court said it's up to each person to make sure their gun is legal.[6]

In 1993, the Court of Appeal upheld a sentence of nine months in jail plus two years probation for the possession of a rifle that, with its folding stock closed, measured 25¾ inches—¼ inch under the legal limit.[7] If you have any question at all about whether your gun is under the limit, measure it carefully!

Cane Guns and Wallet Guns: Guns concealed within canes, crutches, or any type of walking stick (a "cane gun"), or within wallets (a "wallet gun"), if the gun can be fired while it's inside the hidden container.[8]

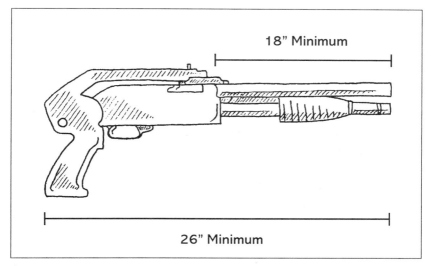

A shotgun must have a barrel of at least 18" and an overall length of at least 26". If it has a folding stock, it must be measured with the stock closed.

Guns "Not Immediately Recognizable": Any gun that is not "immediately recognizable" as a gun.[9]

Zip Guns: A zip gun is any gun that was not imported or manufactured by a licensed company, and which did not have taxes paid on it (this includes "homemade" guns).[11]

Undetectable Guns: A gun whose major parts cannot be detected by a metal detector or recognized by an X-ray machine. Federal law also prohibits these guns, with penalties of a fine and up to five years in prison.[10]

Unconventional Pistols: A gun that does not have a rifled bore and that has a barrel length of less than 18" or an overall length of less than 26".[12]

Machine Guns: A machine gun is a gun which automatically fires more than one shot, without manual reloading, by a single pull of the trigger. The law also includes in the definition of machine gun:[13]

119

1. A frame or receiver which can only be used with a machine gun.

2. Any part or combination of parts that are designed and intended for use in converting a gun to a machine gun.

3. Any gun that the BATF says is "readily convertible" to a machine gun.[14]

Any person who possesses or knowingly transports a machine gun (except as permitted by law) is guilty of a felony/misdemeanor, including a fine of up to $10,000. Any person who intentionally converts a gun into a machine gun, or who sells, offers for sale, or knowingly manufactures a machine gun (except as permitted by law) is guilty of a felony, punishable by four, six, or eight years. Federal law also bans the possession or transfer of machine guns, with penalties of a fine and up to ten years in federal prison.[15]

Assault Weapons: See next chapter on assault weapons.

Guns Greater than .60 Caliber: Guns that fire fixed ammunition greater than .60 caliber, *other than* shotguns, antique rifles, or antique cannons. .60 caliber means 60/100ths of an inch in diameter.

The shotguns can be smooth or rifled bore guns that the Secretary of the Treasury has found particularly suitable for sporting purposes (which means almost any shotgun that can be legally manufactured or sold in the U.S.). An "antique rifle" has the same definition as an "antique gun" (see page 126). An "antique cannon" is any cannon manufactured before January 1, 1899, which has been made incapable of firing *or* where its ammunition is no longer manufactured in the United States and is not readily available in the ordinary channels of commercial trade.

Possession of an illegal large-caliber gun is a felony/misdemeanor including a fine of up to $10,000, and in some cases a felony. Suspended sentences and probation are not allowed. The DOJ issues permits for such guns to certain persons, including motion picture and television studios. See page 129 and Section 12305 for details.[16]

Federal law also prohibits these guns, but the federal standard is anything greater than *.50* caliber. Any person transporting these guns in interstate commerce can be fined and imprisoned for up to five years. Shotguns, antiques, sporting rifles, and non-weapons are exempt from this law.[17]

Imitation Guns: Replicas of guns that look so authentic a reasonable person would think they were real. Any person who buys, sells, transports, or receives an imitation gun can be fined up to $10,000 (there is no jail term). There are exceptions for replicas which will only be used for export from California, in a theatrical production, in a certified or regulated athletic event, in military or civil defense activities, or for public displays authorized by public or private schools. Also excepted are certain replicas of historical or antique guns (see Section 417.2(d)), air guns, spot marker guns, and replicas approved under federal law because they have a marking such as a bright orange plug in the barrel.[18]

Disassembled Guns: For all of the above, and in general, any gun that has been taken apart into pieces, but can be put back together to form one of the above guns, is considered by the law to be a gun.[19]

"Saturday Night Specials" and "Junk" Guns: Many cities have banned the sale of small, often cheaply-made handguns within their city limits. There is no ban on possession, however, and most cities still allow gun dealers to perform private party transfers between gun owners.

Advertising Illegal Guns and Ammunition: If California law prohibits the possession of a type of gun, gun device, or ammunition, you can't advertise that gun, gun device, or ammunition for sale in any way or form.[20]

Illegal Gun Devices

The federal crime bill passed in 1994 bans "large capacity ammunition feeding devices." This is a fancy term for magazines and anything else that hold more than ten rounds of ammunition. The ban affects all magazines and other feeding devices manufactured after September 13, 1994.

Large Capacity Ammunition Feeding Devices: This means any magazine, belt, drum, feed strip or other device that can hold, or be readily restored or converted to hold, more than ten rounds of ammunition. It does not include magazines and other devices manufactured on or before the date the federal crime bill was enacted, September 13, 1994. It also does not include attached tubular magazines or other tubular devices that hold only .22 caliber rimfire ammunition. Possession or transfer of a large capacity ammunition feeding device is a federal offense, punishable by a fine of up to $5,000 and up to five years in prison.[21]

You can keep the magazines, belts, drums, feed strips and other devices you already have, as long as they were manufactured on or before September 13, 1994. You can buy or sell them, or give them away. But you can't possess or transfer any made after September 13, 1994. Federal law requires manufacturers of ammunition feeding devices made after the ban to mark them with a sign, such as a serial number, that indicates when they were manufactured (but this requirement won't get you off the hook if you possess or transfer one made after September 13, 1994 that doesn't have a sign).

The large capacity ammunition feeding device ban does not apply to: government agencies, law enforcement officers on and off duty, certain retired law enforcement officers, nuclear plant security personnel, and testing and experimentation authorized by the Secretary of the Treasury. See Title 18 of the United States Code, Section 922(w) for details.

Camouflaging Firearm Containers: Any container made to enclose a gun so that it is not "readily recognizable" as containing a gun, and which allows the gun to be fired by external controls while it is inside the container. Example: a briefcase with hidden gun that you can fire by pressing a button on its handle. "Camouflaging firearm containers" do not include camouflage covering used while lawfully hunting or while going to or coming from a hunting trip.[22]

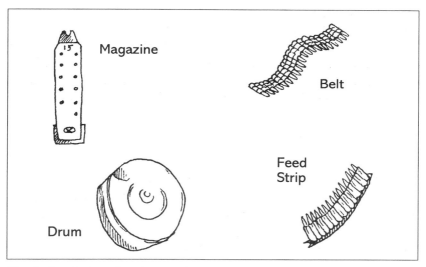

The federal crime law bans all new devices that hold more than ten rounds of ammunition, such as the ones pictured above .

Silencers: A silencer is any device or attachment designed, used, or intended for use in silencing, diminishing (lessening), or muffling the sound a gun makes when it fires. The legal definition also includes any combination of parts, designed or redesigned, and intended for use in assembling or making a silencer, and any part intended only for use in assembling or making a silencer. Any person, firm, or corporation who possesses a silencer is guilty of a felony, including a fine of up to $10,000 in addition to imprisonment in the state prison. There are exceptions for the military, law enforcement, and their suppliers.[23]

Multiburst Trigger Activators: Devices which allow a semiautomatic gun (which normally fires one shot for each pull of the trigger) to fire two or more shots in a burst. Also, manual and power-driven devices which increase the rate of fire of a gun when attached to the gun.[24]

Sniperscopes: A scope that lets you see in the dark. The legal definition is any attachment or device designed for a gun, or adaptable for use on a gun, which allows you to see things at night through the use of a projected infrared light source and an electronic telescope. Possession of a sniperscope is a misdemeanor. There are exceptions for law enforcement officers, and people who possess and use a sniperscope solely for scientific research or educational purposes.[25]

Masks: It's a felony/misdemeanor to carry a gun in a public place or on any public street while you are masked to hide your identity. This law does not apply to: licensed hunters while actually engaged in lawful hunting, or while going directly to or coming directly from the hunting trip; authorized participants in entertainment productions or other lawfully organized events, while performing or rehearsing, so long as they have unloaded guns or guns loaded with blanks; full-time peace officers in the performance of their duties; and persons summoned by such peace officers to assist the officer in making arrests or preserving the peace, while those persons are actually assisting the officer.[26]

Body Armor: Body armor (such as a bulletproof vest) is not illegal to have or wear. But note that if you wear a body vest, defined as any bullet resistant material intended to provide ballistic and trauma protection for the wearer, while committing or attempting to commit a violent felony, your sentence for the underlying crime may be increased by one, two, or five extra years.[27]

Illegal Ammunition

Flechette Darts: A small dart that can be fired from a gun, and that is approximately one inch in length with tail fins that take up five-sixteenths of an inch of the body.[28]

Explosive Bullets: Bullets that contain or carry an explosive agent.[29]

Tracer Ammunition: Ammunition that leaves a trail of light produced by burning material so the shooter can trace the path of the projectile. Tracer ammunition made for shotguns, however, is legal. Possession of illegal tracer ammunition is a felony/misdemeanor; sale and transport is a felony, punishable by two, three, or four years in the state prison. Suspended sentences and probation are not allowed. The DOJ issues permits for such ammunition to certain persons, including motion picture and television studios. See Section 12305 for details.[30]

Armor-Piercing Bullets: This means *handgun* ammunition designed primarily to penetrate a body vest or body shield. See Section 12323 for detailed definition. Ammunition used in a rifle is still considered handgun ammunition if the ammunition is *principally* (mainly) used in pistols and revolvers. Possession by any person, firm, or corporation is a felony/misdemeanor, including a fine of up to $5,000. Manufacture, import, sale, offering for sale, and transport is a felony. There are exceptions for people with permits from the DOJ (see Section 12305), law enforcement laboratories, and the military. Also, it is legal to possess, import, sell, and transport armor-piercing bullets from which the propellent (powder) has been removed and the primer has been permanently deactivated.[31]

Ammunition Greater than .60 Caliber: Fixed ammunition greater than .60 caliber, except shotgun ammunition (single projectile or shot). Possession is a misdemeanor for the first offense, and a felony/misdemeanor for the second and following offenses. Suspended sentences and probation are not allowed. The DOJ issues permits for such ammunition to certain persons, including motion picture and television studios. See Section 12305 for details.[32]

Exceptions

The exceptions listed below let you possess any of the above guns, ammunition, or gun devices, *except for* machine guns, large capacity ammunition feeding devices, sniper-scopes, tracer ammunition, and armor-piercing bullets. The following guns, gun devices, and ammunition are legal to possess under California law:

"Antique Guns": Guns whose model was manufactured in the year 1898 or before, and which were not designed (or later modified) to use rimfire or conventional center fire fixed ammunition. It does not matter whether your actual gun was made after 1898, so long as that model of gun was being manufactured in 1898 or earlier. Examples are certain models of matchlock, flintlock, and percussion cap guns. Also, guns which use fixed ammunition if they were actually manufactured in 1898 or earlier, and if they use ammunition which is no longer manufactured in the United States and is not readily available from ordinary commercial sources.[33]

"Curios or Relics": Historic or rare guns or ammunition of special interest to gun collectors. To fall under this exception, the collectors must be licensed as collectors under federal law. See Title 27 of the Code of Federal Regulations, Section 178.11, for the legal definition of curios or relics.[34]

A person prohibited from possessing a gun or ammunition under California law (including certain minors) cannot possess a curio or relic. If one of these persons inherits a curio or relic from a deceased person, they may hold legal title to it so long as they sell or give it away within one year;

but at no time can they have it in their actual physical possession.

Federal Unconventional Guns: Guns specified in Title 26 of the United States Code, Section 5845(e) when possessed by persons who have a permit to possess them under the federal Gun Control Act of 1968 (P.L. 90-618) and the regulations thereunder. Called "any other weapon" by federal law, they include pistols with a smooth bore designed to fire a shotgun shell, guns with combination rifle and shotgun barrels, and others. This exception does not make it legal for anyone to possess a pen gun.[35]

A person prohibited from possessing a gun or ammunition under California law (including certain minors) cannot possess one of these guns. If one of these persons inherits such a gun from a deceased person, they may hold legal title to it so long as they sell or give it away within one year; but at no time can they have it in their actual physical possession.

Museums: Guns and gun devices kept by museums and historical societies which are open to the public, if they are kept secure and the guns are unloaded.[36]

Entertainment Productions: Guns and gun devices, other than short-barreled shotguns or short-barreled rifles, that are kept or used for motion picture production or other entertainment events. The person possessing the gun or gun device must be an authorized participant in the production or an authorized employee or agent of the production company[37]

Prop and Museum Providers: Guns and ammunition, other than short-barreled shotguns and short-barreled rifles, manufactured, imported, possessed, sold, or lent by persons in the business of providing guns and ammunition only to entertainment production companies and museums (as described above), when engaging in transactions with the production companies or museums.[38]

127

Law Enforcement Agencies and Their Suppliers: Guns and ammunition, including short-barreled shotguns and short-barreled rifles, that are sold to, purchased by, or possessed by law enforcement agencies for use in their official duties, and possessed by authorized, regular, full-time peace officers while on duty. Also, guns and ammunition except for short-barreled shotguns and short-barreled rifles that are manufactured, imported, possessed, sold, or lent by persons who are in the business of supplying such weapons to law enforcement agencies, when engaging in transactions with those agencies.[39]

Permits Issued by the Department of Justice

Short-Barreled Shotgun or Short-Barreled Rifle Permits: You can apply to the DOJ for a special permit if you have a reason to possess a short-barreled shotgun or short-barreled rifle, such as for a movie prop. You may also need a federal permit, if you want to transport them in interstate commerce (contact the Bureau of Alcohol, Tobacco and Firearms).[40]

The DOJ will issue a permit for the manufacture, possession, transportation, or sale of short-barreled shotguns or short-barreled rifles if it finds that granting the permit will not endanger the public safety. Applicants must be 18 years of age or older, and must show that good cause exists for granting the permit. See Sections 12095-12098 for details. There are only two grounds that are considered "good cause" for a short-barreled shotgun or rifle permit:

1. The guns will be used only as props for movie, television, video production, or other entertainment events, and only with blank cartridges.

2. The applicant is a gun dealer or manufacturer who is licensed under federal law, and who will supply the guns to law enforcement agencies or the military.

Machine Gun Permit Holders: There are two exceptions to the prohibition on machine guns: certain law enforcement agencies and the military, and people with machine gun permits. The DOJ can issue a permit for the possession, manufacture, and/or transportation of machine guns to any person over 18 who can show "good cause." The law does not define what "good cause" would be; the people who have the best chance of getting a permit are people in the gun business who will supply machine guns to law enforcement agencies and the military, and people who supply props for entertainment productions. See Sections 12230-12251 for details.[41]

Dangerous Weapon Permit Details: The DOJ issues permits for the possession, transport, and sale of dangerous weapons including short-barreled guns, machine guns, assault weapons, and destructive devices (such as the two permits described above). In general, the DOJ will only grant a permit to someone who will use the weapon commercially or in connection with the government. Examples are people in the gun business, government contractors, gunsmiths, and government agencies, as long as they meet certain criteria. Collectors can get a permit to possess destructive devices (such as large-caliber guns and ammunition) but can't get a permit to possess short-barreled guns, machine guns, or assault weapons. See Title 11 of the California Code of Regulations, Sections 971-972.3 for details.

Endnotes

1. Penal Code § 12020(a).

2. People v. Lanham (1991) 230 Cal.App.3d 1396, 1405; People v. Valencia (1989) 214 Cal.App.3d 1410, 1416.

3. Penal Code §§ 12001.5, 12020(a), (c)(1), (c)(2).

4. 18 U.S.C. §§ 922(a)(4), 924(a); 26 U.S.C. § 5845(f).

5. People v. Stinson (1970) 8 Cal.App.3d 497, 500; People v. Rooney (1993) 17 Cal.App.4th 1207, 1212; 27 C.F.R. § 179.11 (see "Firearm").

6. People v. Valencia (1989) 214 Cal.App.3d 1410, 1416.

7. People v. Rooney (1993) 17 Cal.App.4th 1207, 1212.

8. Penal Code § 12021(a), (c)(4), (c)(5).

9. Penal Code § 12021(a).

10. Penal Code § 12020(a), (c)(22); 18 U.S.C. § 922(p), 924(e).

11. Penal Code § 12020(a), (c)(10).

12. Penal Code § 12020(a), (c)(12); 18 U.S.C. §§ 922 (a)(4), 924(a).

13. Penal Code § 12200.

14. *See* 26 U.S.C. Ch. 53 (§ 5801, et seq.).

15. Penal Code § 12220; 18 U.S.C. §§ 922(o), 924(a)(2).

16. Penal Code §§ 12301(a)(3); 12303, et seq.; 12311; 27 CFR 179.11.

17. 18 U.S.C. §§ 922(a)(4), 924(a); 26 U.S.C. § 5845(f).

18. Penal Code § 417.2; *See also* 15 U.S.C. § 5001.

19. People v. Hale (1974) 43 Cal.App.3d 353, 356.

20. Penal Code § 12020.5.

21. 18 U.S.C. §§ 921(a)(31), 922(w), 924(a)(1)(b).

22. Penal Code § 12020(a), (c)(9).

23. Penal Code §§ 12500-12520.

24. Penal Code § 12020(a), (c)(23).

25. Penal Code § 468.

26. Penal Code § 12040.

27. Penal Code § 12022.2.

28. Penal Code § 12020(a), (c)(6).

29. Penal Code § 12020(a).

30. Penal Code §§ 12020(b)(6), 12301(a)(1), 12303, 12303.6, 12311.

31. Penal Code §§ 12320-12325.

32. Penal Code §§ 12304, 12311.

33. Penal Code § 12020(b)(5); *See also* 26 U.S.C. § 5845(g).

34. Penal Code § 12020(b)(7); 18 U.S.C. § 921, et seq. (and regulations thereunder).

35. Penal Code § 12020(b)(8).

36. Penal Code § 12020(b)(9).

37. Penal Code § 12020(b)(10).

38. Penal Code § 12020(b)(11).

39. Penal Code § 12020(b)(1), (b)(12), (c)(13).

40. Penal Code §§ 12020(b)(2), 12095-12098.

41. *See also* 18 U.S.C. § 922(o).

Chapter 8: What Are the Laws on Assault Weapons?

What Is an Assault Weapon? When people think of an assault weapon, they usually think of a rifle that is semiautomatic (fires one shot for each pull of the trigger, without manual reloading), has a magazine that holds a relatively high number of medium-power rounds of ammunition, and is small enough to be able to wield easily. They think of guns that are semiautomatic versions of fully automatic (machine gun) military rifles. However, the law has a different definition of "assault weapon," which is explained below. Knowing this definition is crucial if you have or want to have a gun that might be considered an assault weapon. The law also includes some pistols and shotguns in the definition of assault weapon.

Assault weapons are a highly-regulated category of guns under both federal and California law; you have to follow both sets of laws. If you think you might own an assault weapon, or you are considering buying a semiautomatic rifle, pistol, or shotgun that has a high-capacity magazine or other assault weapon features, you should read this chapter carefully. Also, see page 122 for the laws on high capacity magazines.

Federal Assault Weapon Ban

Fed
Federal Law

The federal government began regulating assault weapons with the 1994 crime bill. The federal definition of "assault weapon" lists some guns by name, but is mostly based on the *features* a gun has and *when* it was made. If you or your gun do not fall under an exception, the possession or transfer of an assault weapon is a federal offense punishable by a fine of up to $5,000 and up to five years in prison.[1]

The following guns are considered "assault weapons" under federal law:

Rifles

Any semiautomatic rifle that can accept a detachable magazine and that has at least two of these features:

- ❑ A folding or telescoping stock.

- ❑ A pistol grip that protrudes conspicuously beneath the action of the gun.

- ❑ A bayonet mount.

- ❑ A flash suppressor or threaded barrel designed to accommodate a flash suppressor.

- ❑ A grenade launcher.

Pistols

Any semiautomatic pistol that can accept a detachable magazine and that has at least two of these features:

- ❑ An ammunition magazine that attaches to the pistol outside of the pistol grip.

- ❑ A threaded barrel capable of accepting a barrel extender, flash suppressor, forward handgrip, or silencer.

- ❑ A manufactured weight of 50 ounces or more when the pistol is unloaded.

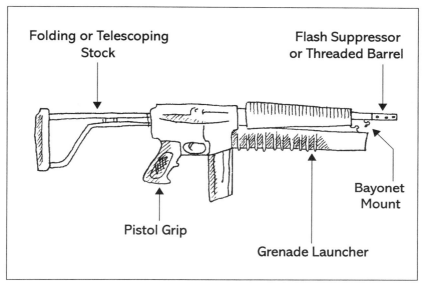

Folding or Telescoping Stock

Flash Suppressor or Threaded Barrel

Bayonet Mount

Pistol Grip

Grenade Launcher

The 1994 federal crime bill banned all new semiautomatic rifles that have a detachable magazine and at least two of the above features.

❑ A shroud that is attached to the barrel (or partially or completely encircles it) that permits the shooter to hold the gun with the nontrigger hand without being burned.

❑ A semiautomatic version of an automatic gun.

Shotguns

Any semiautomatic shotgun that has at least two of these features:

❑ A folding or telescoping stock.

❑ A pistol grip that protrudes conspicuously beneath the action of the gun.

❑ A fixed magazine capacity in excess of 5 rounds.

❑ An ability to accept a detachable magazine.

Guns Listed by Name

The following guns, and copies or duplicates of these guns, in any caliber, are assault weapons under federal law:

1. Norinco, Mitchell, and Poly Technologies Avtomat Kalashnikovs (all models).
2. Action Arms Israeli Military Industries UZI and Galil.
3. Beretta Ar70 (SC-70).
4. Colt AR-15.
5. Fabrique National FN/FAL, FN/LAR, and FNC.
6. SWD M-10, M-11, M-11/9, and M-12.
7. Steyr AUG.
8. INTRATEC TEC-9, TEC-DC9, and TEC-22.
9. Revolving cylinder shotguns, such as (or similar to) the Street Sweeper and Striker 12.

Exceptions to the Federal Ban

The federal assault weapon ban does *not* apply to:

❑ Guns manufactured on or before the date the federal crime bill was enacted, September 13, 1994.

❑ Guns that are manually operated by bolt, pump, lever, or slide action.

❑ Semiautomatic rifles that cannot accept detachable magazines that hold more than 5 rounds of ammunition.

❑ Semiautomatic shotguns that cannot hold more than 5 rounds of ammunition in a fixed or detachable magazine.

❑ Guns that are considered antique firearms under federal law (see definition on page 126).

❑ Guns that have been fixed so they can never fire (guns "rendered permanently inoperable").

❑ Any gun listed in Title 22 of the United States Code, Section 922, Appendix A, as such guns were manufactured on October 1, 1993. Also, replicas and duplicates of these guns. These guns are mostly hunting and historic guns, and are not typical assault weapons.

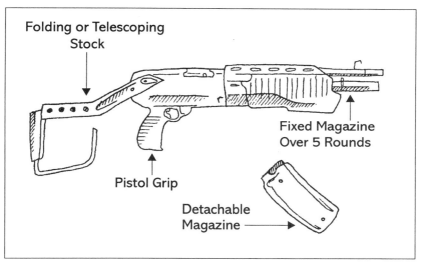

Folding or Telescoping Stock

Fixed Magazine Over 5 Rounds

Pistol Grip

Detachable Magazine

The 1994 federal crime bill banned all new semiautomatic shotguns that have at least two of the above features.

Federal law lets you keep the assault weapons you already have, as long as they were manufactured on or before September 13, 1994. You can buy or sell them, or give them away. But you can't possess or transfer (sell, give, lend, etc.) any assault weapons made after September 13, 1994. Federal law requires manufacturers of assault weapons made after this date to mark them with a serial number that shows the date the guns were manufactured (but this requirement won't get you off the hook if you possess or transfer one made after September 13, 1994 that doesn't have a date).

The federal assault weapon ban does not apply to: government agencies, law enforcement officers on and off duty, certain retired law enforcement officers, nuclear plant security, and testing and experimentation authorized by the Secretary of the Treasury. See Title 18 of the United States Code, Section 922(v), for details.

California Assault Weapon Ban

In 1989, the State Legislature passed the Roberti-Roos Assault Weapons Control Act, which puts assault weapons into a separate group of guns. California regulates assault weapons by make and model of gun, rather than by the features a gun has. The Legislature has made a list of all guns that are "assault weapons." The guns on this list have severe restrictions on sales, ownership, and use, and more guns can be added to the list in the future. To legally have one of these guns, you must register it within 90 days after it gets on the list (currently there is a grace period; see below).

List of Assault Weapons

California maintains a list of all guns that are "assault weapons." All the following guns are assault weapons.[2] Guns marked with an asterisk (*) were placed on the list on January 1, 1992. Guns without an asterisk were placed on the list on June 1, 1989.

Rifles

The following semiautomatic rifles:

1. All AK series including, but not limited to, the following models:
   *Made in China AK, AKM, AKS, AK47, AK47S, 56, 56S, 84S, and 86S.
   *Norinco 56, 56S, 84S, and 86S.
   *Poly Technologies AKS and AK47.
   *MAADI AK47 and ARM.

All other guns in the AK "series." This means all guns, regardless of manufacturer, that are only variations of the above AK guns except for minor differences.[4]

2. UZI and Galil.
3. Beretta AR-70.
4. *CETME Sporter.
5. Colt AR-15 series.

    In addition to the Colt AR-15 itself, the word "series" means all guns, regardless of manufacturer, that are only variations of the Colt AR-15 except for minor differences.[4]

6. Daewoo K-1, K-2, Max 1, Max 2, *AR 100, *AR110C.
7. Fabrique Nationale FAL, LAR, FNC, *308 Match, and *Sporter.
8. MAS 223.
9. HK-91, *HK-93, HK-94, and HK-PSG-1.
10. The following MAC types:

    *RPB Industries Inc. sM10 and sM11.

    *SWD Incorporated M11.

11. SKS with detachable magazine.
12. SIG AMT, PE-57, *SG 550, and *SG 551.
13. Springfield Armory BM59 and SAR-48.
14. Sterling MK-6
15. Steyer AUG.
16. Valmet M62S, M71S, and M78S.
17. Armalite AR-180.
18. Bushmaster Assault Rifle.
19. Calico M-900.
20. *J&R ENG M-68.
21. Weaver Arms Nighthawk.

Pistols

1. UZI.
2. Encom MP-9 and MP-45.
3. The following MAC types:

    *RPB Industries Inc. sM10 and sM11.

    *SWD Incorporated M-11.

    *Advance Armament Inc. M-11

*Military Armament Corp. Ingram M-11

4.   Intratec TEC-9.
5.   *Sites Spectre.
6.   Sterling MK-7.
7.   *Calico M-950.
8.   *Bushmaster Pistol.

Shotguns

1.   Franchi SPAS 12 and LAW 12.
2.   *Striker 12.
3.   *The Streetsweeper type S/S Inc. SS/12.

Guns Added by Courts

Courts can add guns to the list by declaring a gun to be an "assault weapon."

How Are Guns Added to the List?

There are two ways that guns are added to the California list: the Legislature can pass an amendment to Section 12276 which adds a gun to the list, and the Attorney General can ask the superior court to rule that a gun is an assault weapon. The Attorney General may do so when gun manufacturers attempt to get around the assault weapon laws by renaming or slightly changing an assault weapon.[3]

After the Attorney General files a petition to have a gun declared an assault weapon, the court will *temporarily suspend* that gun's manufacture, sale, distribution, transportation, and importation into California, as well as the right to give or lend it. The Attorney General must give notice of the temporary suspension to law enforcement agencies, certain persons in the gun business, industry and consumer gun publications, and any persons who have requested to receive this type of notice. A notice must also be published in 10 different newspapers. After notice of the temporary suspension is given, the gun is considered an assault weapon, and the laws against distribution, transport, sale, etc. of the gun apply.

The court then holds a hearing, and will declare the gun to be an assault weapon if the Attorney General proves its case. (Owners of that model of gun can challenge the Attorney General at the hearing with the court's permission; see Section 12276.5 for details.) If the gun is declared an assault weapon, the Attorney General prepares a description and illustration of the assault weapon, and distributes it to all law enforcement agencies. The Attorney General must also prepare a new list of assault weapons that is filed with the Secretary of State and published in the California Code of Regulations. The list must be updated within 90 days of a new gun being added to the list.

Remember that even though the Attorney General can only have a gun added to the list by following this procedure, the State Legislature can add a gun to the list at any time simply by passing a bill which adds a gun to the list of assault weapons. New laws usually take effect on January 1 of the next year, but certain "urgency" legislation can take effect as soon as the governor signs it.

How Can You Keep Track of Guns that Are Added to the List?

❑ One way is to read gun magazines and newspapers that publish news about assault weapons, and to inquire at your local gun store. The problem with this method is that you cannot be completely sure their information is accurate.

❑ Another way is to read the Penal Code and the California Code of Regulations on a regular basis, to see whether your gun has been placed on the list by a court or by the Legislature. Your local law library, usually located in county courthouses, should have materials which allow you to check on this. However, you may not have access to a set of these books that is updated often enough to be safe. Also, you have only 90 days to register a gun after it is declared to be an assault weapon, and publication might not take place within the 90 days.

❑ The best way is to ask the DOJ. Their address is: Department of Justice, Firearms Program, P.O. Box 820200, Sacramento, CA 90403-0200. Telephone: 916/227-3695, Monday through Friday, 8:00 a.m. to 5:00 p.m. They will answer your questions and can send you an assault weapon registration card.

❑ The more likely it is that your gun may be declared an assault weapon, the more you need to stay current with the law.

California regulates assault weapons by placing them on a list. Guns are listed by make and model. Listed guns have strict limitations on possession and use.

How to Register Your Assault Weapon

The list in this book is a complete list of California assault weapons at the time this book was printed. All guns have been on the list over 90 days. No guns have been added to the list since January 1, 1992.

When Your Gun Has Been on the List for Over 90 Days: If you have a gun that is on the list of assault weapons, and it has been more than 90 days since your gun was added to the list, the DOJ *currently* (at the time this book was printed) will let you register it as long as you lawfully got the gun before it was placed on the list. If you got your gun after it was placed on the list, you cannot register it but you can apply for a special permit to possess the gun. If you do not apply for the permit, or you apply and are denied, you must relinquish (give up) your gun to the police or sheriff's department. If you continue to possess the assault weapon without registration or a permit, you can be charged with a serious crime (see below).

When Your Gun Has Just Been Added to the List: If you possess a gun which has been added to the list, you have 90 days to register the gun with the DOJ. You must have lawfully owned the gun before it was added to the list in order to register it.

To register your gun, contact the California Department of Justice (see address and telephone number on page 140). They will send you a registration card by mail. You must complete the card, get your thumbprint taken for the card (at your local law enforcement agency or the DMV), and return the card to the DOJ with a check or money order for $20. Family members living in the same household can register assault weapons as joint owners, but the $20 fee applies per person. Persons under 18 and persons who are prohibited from possessing a gun cannot possess or register assault weapons.[5]

Alternatives to Registration: If you lawfully possessed a gun before it was declared to be an assault weapon, you may also, *within the 90 day grace period:* sell the gun to a licensed gun dealer, take the gun out of the state, obtain a special permit for the gun, or render the gun permanently inoperable (make it so it can never fire again).

Person Moving to California: If you lawfully possess an assault weapon before moving to California, you must do one of the following two things with it:[6]

1. *Before* bringing the weapon into California, get a special permit from the DOJ to possess it in California (see below for special permit details); or

2. Deliver the weapon to a licensed gun dealer in California according to federal law.[7] Then, apply for a special permit from the DOJ. If you receive it, the dealer will give the gun to you.

How Can You Lawfully Use Your Assault Weapon?

A person who has registered an assault weapon in California can possess and use it only under the following conditions:[8]

Places: An assault weapon can only be possessed and used at:

❑ Your place of residence, your place of business (that you own), or at other property you own. Also, at property owned by another person with that person's express permission. Examples of such use include self-defense and display.

❑ A target range of a public or private club or organization that is organized for the purpose of target shooting.

❑ A target range which has a regulatory or business license, for the purpose of target shooting at that range. (A designated shooting area, for example, does not have a regulatory or business license.)

❑ A shooting club which is licensed under the Fish and Game Code.

❑ While attending an exhibition, display, or educational project about guns, which is sponsored by or approved by a law enforcement agency or a nationally or state recognized entity (company, organization, or group) that promotes or fosters gun training or education.

❑ On publicly owned land if the possession and use of an assault weapon is *specifically permitted* by the agency that manages the land.

Transport: You can transport your assault weapon between any of the above places, or to a licensed gun dealer to get the gun serviced or repaired. While transporting the gun, you must follow the same rules as for the Locked Container in Motor Vehicle exception to the concealed gun law (see page 49). An acceptable way to transport the gun is to keep it unloaded, in a locked container in a motor vehicle other than the glove box or utility compartment. The gun must also be in a locked container when it is carried to and from the vehicle. A secure gun case that is completely enclosed and locked by a padlock, key lock, or combination lock is an acceptable locked container.

Additional Places and Uses by Special Permit: If you get a special permit for an assault weapon (see below) that lets you keep it in additional places and use it in additional ways, you may keep and use it as specified in the permit.

Special Permit Available

The DOJ issues a special assault weapon permit for two types of persons:[9]

1. Persons who lawfully acquired an assault weapon before it was placed on the list and who want to use it in a different way than normally allowed by law, such as in an entertainment production. This permit will allow the use of the weapon in the way(s) specified in the permit.

2. Persons who want to acquire a gun that is already on the list of assault weapons. This permit will allow a person to legally get an assault weapon.

The permit procedure is the same as for a machine gun permit. In general, the DOJ will only grant a permit to someone who will use the assault weapon commercially or in connection with the government. See page 129 for details.

Local Laws on Assault Weapons

A few California cities, including Los Angeles, Palo Alto, and Stockton, have banned assault weapons within their cities, usually making possession of an assault weapon a misdemeanor. If you have a semiautomatic gun that has any features common to assault weapons in general, read your local codes and ordinances to find out whether your city or county has an assault weapon law, and contact local government officials to inquire whether the local law remains in effect after passage of the statewide Roberti-Roos law.

Punishment for Violating Assault Weapon Laws

Sale, Transport, Etc.: Any person who manufactures, causes to be manufactured, distributes, transports, imports into California, keeps for sale, offers or exposes for sale, or gives or lends any assault weapon, except as allowed under the assault weapon laws, is guilty of a felony punishable by four, six, or eight years in the state prison. Any person who transfers, lends, sells, or gives an assault weapon to a minor will receive an additional sentence of one year.[10]

Possession: Any person in California who possesses an assault weapon, except as allowed under the assault weapon laws, is guilty of a felony/misdemeanor.[11]

A first-time violation of this possession law is only an infraction, punishable by a fine of between $350 and $500 and no jail term, if all of the following applies to you:

❑ You present proof that you lawfully possessed the gun prior to the time it was added to the list of assault weapons, but you did not register it.

❑ You have registered the assault weapon between the time it was added to the list and the time you go to court, or you have relinquished it (given it up) by giving it to the police.

❑ You have followed the rules for possessing an assault weapon only in certain places and under certain conditions (see above).

If the above is true, your gun will be returned to you unless the court rules, at a hearing, that the gun poses a threat to the public safety and must be destroyed. If a hearing is scheduled, you will be given notice of the hearing's date, time, and place.

Exceptions to Assault Weapon Laws

Possession Before 90-day Grace Period Expires: You may possess an assault weapon during the 90-day period after it was added to the list of assault weapons, if you are over 18, are not in a group of persons prohibited from having a gun, and you lawfully possessed the gun before the date it was added to the list. The date the gun was added to the list means either: the date an amendment to the law passed by the State Legislature became effective, or the date the

145

Attorney General added the gun to the list by getting a court order, whichever is earlier. During the grace period, you must comply with all the other assault weapon rules, including the places where the assault weapon may be possessed.[12]

Transfer to Gun Dealer for Sale or Repair: You may transfer an assault weapon to a licensed gun dealer, to sell it to the dealer or to have it serviced or repaired, without violating the law against transferring assault weapons. Before making the transfer, you must have either registered the assault weapon or have a special permit for it. If you are having the gun repaired, the gun dealer will transfer the gun to a gunsmith for you. You cannot transfer the gun directly to a gunsmith for service or repair unless the gunsmith is a licensed gun dealer. See page 164 for the definition of a licensed gun dealer.[13]

Relinquishing (Giving Up) Your Assault Weapon: If you have an unregistered assault weapon, and you cannot register it because you got it after it was placed on the list of assault weapons, or you don't want to apply for a special permit for it, or if you no longer wish to have it for any other reason, you can arrange *in advance* to give the weapon to the police or sheriff's department (relinquishing an illegal assault weapon at the time you are caught with it won't work). The way the law is written is unclear, but you probably won't be prosecuted for unlawful possession of an assault weapon if you relinquish your gun in advance. You must transport the gun to the police or sheriff according to the same rules as for the Locked Container in Motor Vehicle exception to the concealed gun law (see page 49).[14]

Lending Assault Weapons: You may lend your assault weapon to another person if you follow these rules:[15]

❑ You lawfully possess the gun and have registered it.

❑ The person you are lending it to is over 18 and is not in a class of persons who are prohibited from having a gun (see Chapter 1).

❑ You stay in the presence of the person you lent the gun to while he or she has the gun.

❑ You lend the gun at one of the following three places:

1. On a target range that has a regulatory or business license, for the purpose of target shooting at that range. (A designated shooting area, for example, does not have a regulatory or business license.)
2. On a target range of a public or private club or organization that is organized for the purpose of target shooting.
3. While attending an exhibition, display, or educational project about guns, which is sponsored by or approved by a law enforcement agency or a nationally or state recognized entity (company, organization, or group) that promotes or fosters gun training or education.

The person you lent the assault weapon to may possess the gun and return it to you without violating the laws against possessing or transferring assault weapons, as long as he or she follows the above rules.

Executors or Administrators of Estates: An executor or administrator of an estate that includes an assault weapon may dispose of (transfer) the weapon, as long as the weapon is registered, the transfer is authorized by the probate court, and the transfer is permitted by the other assault weapon laws. The executor or administrator may possess the gun only at his or her residence, place of business, or other property owned by him or her, or on property owned by another with the owner's express permission; or, as authorized by the probate court.[16]

Out-of-State Competitive Shooters: If you don't live in California, and you want to use your assault weapon in a shooting competition in this state, you can possess an assault weapon here by following certain rules. See Section 12280(k) for details.

Law Enforcement and Military; Sales to Same: Certain law enforcement agencies and the military may possess and use assault weapons. Certain persons may manufacture and sell assault weapons to such agencies.[17]

Warning About Modifying Your Gun

If you have a gun that is not on the list of assault weapons, and you modify the gun in such a way that it matches a gun on the list, your gun will be considered an assault weapon.[18] For example, you can't adapt an SKS rifle that originally came with a fixed 10-round magazine to accept a 30-round detachable magazine. One of the rifles on California's list of assault weapons is "SKS with detachable magazine."

The court case that established this rule, *People v. Dingman*, is currently under review by the California Supreme Court. The law in this area may change shortly as a result.

Endnotes

1. 18 U.S.C. §§ 922(v), 924(a)(1)(B).
2. Penal Code § 12276.
3. Penal Code § 12276.5.
4. Penal Code § 12276(e).
5. Penal Code § 12285(a), (d).
6. Penal Code § 12285(b)(2).
7. *See* 18 U.S.C. Chapter 44 (§ 921, et seq.) and regulations thereunder.
8. Penal Code § 12285(c).
9. Penal Code § 12286.
10. Penal Code § 12280(a).
11. Penal Code § 12280(b).
12. Penal Code § 12280(e), (l).
13. Penal Code §§ 12285(b)(1), 12290(b).
14. Penal Code § 12288.
15. Penal Code § 12280(i), (j).
16. Penal Code § 12280(g), (h).
17. Penal Code §§ 12280(d), (f), 12287.
18. People v. Dingman (1996) 47 Cal.App.4th 1068, rev. granted.

Chapter 9: How Can You Transfer or Dispose of Your Gun?

How to Transfer Your Gun

To "transfer" a gun means to sell it, lend it, give it to someone, or anything else you do that puts your gun into the hands of another person. The person you transfer a gun to is called the "transferee."

There are two main rules for transferring guns; this book refers to the rules as Rule 1 and Rule 2. Rule 1 states that unless you are a licensed gun dealer, you may transfer guns only infrequently. This rule is designed to stop you from conducting a gun dealing business without being properly licensed.

Rule 2 requires you to use the services of a licensed gun dealer to complete a gun transfer (or, if you live in a small county, you may use the county sheriff's department). This rule is designed to ensure that all the gun transfer requirements are followed when you transfer a gun, such as the 15-day waiting period and background check (see page 7).

You must follow *both* Rule 1 *and* Rule 2. Both of these rules have exceptions, which are discussed below. For additional laws that apply to transferring guns and ammunition to minors, see the section, "When Can a Minor Have a Gun?," starting on page 28.

Rule 1: Infrequent Gun Transfers Only

Under California law, you may transfer guns only infrequently, unless you are a licensed gun dealer or you fall under an exception. Violation of this law is a misdemeanor.[1]

"Infrequent Transfer" Rule: You must conduct less than six handgun transactions in each calendar year (January 1–December 31), and you may transfer rifles and shotguns only "occasionally and without regularity." A "transaction" is the transfer of *any number* of handguns at one time to one person.[2]

The rule for rifles and shotguns, that you may transfer them only "occasionally and without regularity," is somewhat vague. If you believe you might be regularly transferring rifles or shotguns, you should contact the DOJ and/or consult a lawyer about whether or not you need a dealer's license. You should also check to see if an exception would be more appropriate for you, such as the exception for "Gun Show Traders."

Exceptions to Rule 1: In addition to infrequent transfers, you may transfer guns in the following situations:

❑ **"Gun Show Trader" Program:** Gun Show Traders may transfer up to 75 used rifles and shotguns at gun shows each year. They need a federal firearms license and a certificate of eligibility from the DOJ. Contact the DOJ for details, and/or see Penal Code Sections 12070(b)(5) and

12071(a)(4), and Title 11 of the California Code of Regulations, Sections 980-985.

❏ **"Antique Guns" and Long "Curios or Relics":** Unloaded antique guns and curios and relics that are not handguns are exempt from both Rule 1 and Rule 2. You may transfer them freely. See page 126 for the definitions of "antique guns" and "curios or relics."[7]

❏ **Other Exceptions:** There are other exceptions that apply to certain detailed situations, including spousal transfers, transfer of guns received upon death, entertainment prop suppliers, and more. If you need to transfer guns and the above exceptions are not sufficient, see Sections 12070, 12076, and 12078, and/or consult a lawyer.

Rule 2: You Must Use a Licensed Gun Dealer to Complete a Gun Transfer

If you want to transfer your gun to someone (or if you want someone to transfer their gun to you), and neither of you is a licensed gun dealer, you must use the services of a licensed gun dealer to deliver the gun to the transferee. If you live in a small county, your sheriff's department may also deliver the gun. These types of transfers are called "private party transfers."

You may fall under an exception. If so, you don't have to use a licensed gun dealer or sheriff's department; see below.

A violation of Rule 2 is a felony/misdemeanor for handgun transfers, and a misdemeanor for rifle and shotgun transfers. After a misdemeanor conviction for illegally transferring a handgun, you can't have a gun for 10 years. If you are in a prohibited group or have certain prior convictions, violation is a felony punishable by two, three, or four years.[3]

Procedure for "Private Party Transfer" Using a Licensed Gun Dealer[4]

1. Bring your gun, along with the transferee, to a licensed gun dealer (such as a gun store).

2. If you are in doubt as to whether the store or dealer is properly licensed, look for a local city or county retail firearms dealer license, which must be displayed at the store where it can easily be seen. Or, ask to see the licenses and certificates listed on page 164.

3. The same rules apply to the transferee as apply to a person buying a gun: the same form must be filled out, there is a 15-day waiting period during which the DOJ checks the transferee's background, the transferee must show proof of identification and age, and the transferee must show the dealer a basic firearms safety certificate to receive a handgun (see page 7 for details). Additional information that must be supplied to the gun dealer is the name and address of the person transferring the gun.

4. The gun dealer will keep the gun during the waiting period. After the waiting period is up, if the transferee has completed all the requirements, the gun dealer will deliver the gun to the transferee.

5. The gun dealer may charge the transferee the standard DOJ fee for a background check, plus a fee of up to $10 for processing the transfer.

6. If the dealer cannot legally transfer the gun to the transferee, such as if the transferee fails the background check or is under age, the dealer must immediately return the gun to you, whether or not the waiting period is up.

7. If the dealer cannot legally return the gun to you because you are prohibited by law from having a gun, the dealer must give the gun to the police for disposal.

8. All licensed gun dealers are required by law to process gun transfers between non-dealers properly and promptly.[5]

IKNOW WE'VE BEEN FRIENDS FOR YEARS, BUT THE ONLY WAY I CAN SELL MY GUN TO YOU IS THROUGH A GUN DEALER.

You can't transfer a gun to someone without using the services of a licensed gun dealer or a small county sheriff's department to complete the transfer (see text for exceptions).

Procedure for "Private Party Transfer" Using a Small County Sheriff's Department[6]

1. If you live in a county with a population of less than 200,000, you may use the services of the sheriff's department to transfer a gun. Your county sheriff's department must have chosen to process gun transfers (call them to see whether they perform this service).

2. The procedure is basically the same as the procedure described above for a private party transfer using a licensed gun dealer. Bring your gun, along with the transferee, to the sheriff's department. Before you walk in with the gun, notify a deputy, either by telephone or in person (leaving the unloaded gun locked in the trunk of your car), that you would like to transfer a gun. Then, bring in the gun when they say it is okay. *Do not just walk into the sheriff's department carrying a gun!*

3. The form the transferee must fill out is called a LEFT (Law Enforcement Firearms Transfer); it is the same form as in the dealer's register of sales. During the time the transferee is filling out the form, you must give the gun to the sheriff's department. They will return it to you after the forms have been filled out.

4. There are the same gun transfer requirements as with a gun dealer (including the 15-day waiting period and other requirements; see page 7 for details). Unlike with a gun dealer, however, *you* keep the gun during the waiting period, not the sheriff. After the waiting period is up, you must bring the gun and the transferee back to the sheriff's department. Assuming the transferee has passed the background check and the other requirements, the gun may then be delivered to him or her. When the gun is delivered to the transferee, it must be securely wrapped or in a locked container.

5. The sheriff's department may charge you the standard DOJ fee for a background check, plus a fee based on the sheriff's actual cost of processing the transfer.

Exceptions to Rule 2—When You Can Complete a Gun Transfer without a Licensed Gun Dealer

The following persons may complete gun transfers as indicated below, without having to use a licensed gun dealer or small county sheriff's department to complete the transfer.

Note—15-day Waiting Period Does Not Apply: The 15-day waiting period is a requirement that is imposed directly on dealers and small county sheriff's departments. There is no waiting period requirement for other persons when they deliver guns under an exception to Rule 2.[8]

"Antique Guns" and Long "Curios or Relics": Unloaded antique guns and curios and relics that are not handguns are exempt from both Rule 1 and Rule 2. You may transfer them freely. See page 126 for the definitions of "antique guns" and "curios or relics."[9]

Grandparent/Parent/Child Transfers: Parents and children, and grandparents and grandchildren, may make infrequent gun transfers to each other. "Infrequent" has the same meaning as in Rule 1 (see page 150). The transfers may occur by gift, bequest (will), intestate succession (dying with no will), or by any other means. Note that there are strict laws on transferring a gun to a minor; these are discussed in the section that starts on page 28.

If handguns are transferred under this exception, the transferee must make a report to the DOJ by mail or in person within 30 days of taking possession of the gun(s). Contact the DOJ for a standard form to use for the report. The DOJ will charge the transferee only one fee for taking possession of any number of guns on the same date. Transferees of handguns must also have a basic firearms safety certificate (see page 9).[10]

You can transfer a gun between grandparents, parents, and children without having to use a licensed gun dealer to complete the transfer (see text for important laws on transferring guns to minors).

Spousal Transfers: Spouses can complete gun transfers to one another when they "transmute" (change the nature of) marital property from community property to separate property, or vice versa. Transmutation also includes a transfer of one spouse's separate property to the other spouse's separate property (but it does not include the transfer of community property between spouses when the nature of the property does not change). You can use this exception to complete a gun transfer to your spouse. For a transmutation to be valid, the spouse transferring the gun must sign a statement consenting to the transmutation of that property. Additionally, guns that pass to a surviving spouse upon the death of the other spouse are exempt from Rule 2.

If handguns are transferred under this exception, the transferee must make a report to the DOJ by mail or in person within 30 days of taking possession of the gun(s). Contact the DOJ for a standard form to use for the report. The

DOJ will charge the transferee only one fee for taking possession of any number of guns on the same date. Transferees of handguns from a living spouse must also have a basic firearms safety certificate (page 9).[11]

Loans: You may make infrequent loans of guns to people you personally know. The loans can be for any lawful purpose, and can be for up to 30 days. "Infrequent" has the same meaning as in Rule 1 (see page 150). You may also loan rifles and shotguns to licensed hunters for a period of time up to the duration of that hunting season in which the guns will be used.[12]

Gun Repair: You may transfer a gun to a gunsmith for service or repair.[13]

Transfers to Licensed Persons Outside California: You may transfer guns to persons outside California who are licensed under federal law (such as persons with a Federal Firearms License), if the transfer complies with federal law. As used in this exception, "federal law" refers to Title 18, Chapter 44 of the United States Code (Sections 921 and following) and the associated federal regulations.[14]

Entertainment Prop Suppliers: Prop suppliers may lend unloaded guns or guns with blank cartridges for use solely as props for motion picture, television, or video productions, or for entertainment or theatrical events.[15]

Transfers to Peace Officers: Transfers of guns to properly identified, full-time, paid peace (law enforcement) officers are exempt from both Rule 1 and Rule 2. See Section 12078(a)(1), (a)(2) for details. If you are in doubt whether the person you wish to transfer your gun to is a peace officer who qualifies under this exception, use a licensed gun dealer to complete the transfer.

Transfers to Gun Buy-Back/Turn-In Programs: Transfers of guns to authorized representatives of cities, counties, and state and federal government agencies are exempt from both Rule 1 and Rule 2, when the agencies are acquiring the guns as part of a voluntary program of buying or receiving guns from private individuals.[16]

Other Exceptions: There are other exceptions that apply to certain detailed situations. If you need to complete a gun transfer and the above exceptions are not sufficient, see Sections 12076 and 12078, and/or consult a lawyer.

Other Gun Transfer Rules

Assault Weapon Transfers: With the exception of lending your assault weapon to another person, the only person you can transfer an assault weapon to is a licensed gun dealer. See Chapter 8 for detailed rules on these transfers.

Optional Report to the DOJ: Any person who acquires, owns, or transfers a handgun, and who is exempt from Rule 2 (the requirement that gun transfers be completed by a licensed gun dealer or small county sheriff's department), or who is not otherwise required by law to make a report, can report the acquisition, ownership, or transfer to the DOJ if he or she wishes. A report can also be made by a person who moves out of state with his or her handgun. Contact the DOJ to obtain a standard form on which to make the report. These reports are entirely optional.[17]

Punishment for Transferring a Gun to a Person in a Prohibited Group

If you transfer any gun to someone who is in a group of persons who are prohibited from having a gun, such as someone who has been convicted of a felony (see the section that starts on page 12), and you *know* that this person is in such a group, you are guilty of a felony punishable by two, three, or four years in the state prison.

If you don't *know* the transferee is in a prohibited group, but you *have cause to believe* he or she is, you are guilty of a felony/misdemeanor. Probation will not be granted, except in unusual circumstances. After a misdemeanor conviction for this offense, you can't have a gun for 10 years. If you are in a prohibited group or have certain prior convictions, violation is a felony punishable by two, three, or four years. If the transferred gun is later used in the commission of a felony, you can be sentenced to an additional one, two, or three years.[18]

Here is an example of "having cause to believe": You want to lend your gun to someone, but a friend told you the person you want to lend it to just got out of prison. You have cause to believe the person is in a prohibited group.

If you transfer a gun to a person who is prohibited from having a gun under federal law, and you know or have reason to believe the person is in a prohibited group, you can be fined and imprisoned for up to 10 years in a federal prison.[19]

You can't transfer a gun to a person you know or have cause to believe is not the actual transferee, but who is simply receiving the gun so that he or she can illegally transfer the gun to someone else (a "straw" buyer). Violation is a felony/misdemeanor; after a misdemeanor conviction for this offense, you can't have a gun for 10 years.[20]

How to Dispose of Your Gun

If you no longer wish to own your gun, and there is no one you want to sell or give it to, there is no California law that prevents you from throwing the gun in the trash. This is not recommended, however, because someone might find the gun and use it in a crime. You might be held criminally and civilly responsible, especially if the person who finds your gun is a child or a person who is prohibited from having a gun. The best way to dispose of your gun is to turn it in to your local police or sheriff's department. They will then follow state law procedures for disposing of the gun.

Before taking the gun to the police or sheriff, call ahead to ask how to best bring the gun to them. If you do not call ahead, leave the gun, unloaded, locked in the trunk of your car, and walk in without the gun (be sure to follow the rules for transporting guns—see page 49). Then, bring in the gun when they say it is okay. *Do not just walk into the police or sheriff's department carrying a gun!*

Endnotes

1. Penal Code §§ 12070(a), 12070(b)(4).
2. Penal Code § 12070(b)(4), (c)(1).
3. Penal Code §§ 12072(d), (g)(1), (g)(2), (g)(3)(G), 12021(c)(1).
4. Penal Code § 12082.
5. Penal Code § 12071(b)(5).
6. Penal Code § 12084.
7. Penal Code § 12001(e).
8. Penal Code §§ 12071(b)(3)(A), 12072(c)(1).
9. Penal Code § 12001(e).
10. Penal Code §§ 12078(c), 12076(h).
11. Penal Code §§ 12078(i), (t)(2)(G), 12076(h); Family Code §§ 850, 852.
12. Penal Code § 12078(d), (q).
13. Penal Code § 12078(e).
14. Penal Code § 12078(f).
15. Penal Code § 12078(s).
16. Penal Code § 12078(a)(3).
17. Penal Code § 12078(l).
18. Penal Code §§ 12072(a)(1), (a)(2), (g)(2), (g)(3), (g)(4), 1203(e)(12), (e)(13), 12021(c)(1); Welfare & Institutions Code § 8101(b).
19. 18 U.S.C. §§ 922(d), 924(a)(2).
20. Penal Code §§ 12072(a)(4), (g)(3)(C), 12021(c)(1).

Chapter 10: Other Important Gun Law Issues

A Word About Gun Safety and Legal Reality

Gun Safety: Guns can be valuable instruments. They can provide a means of protecting your safety and the safety of your loved ones. They can also provide a rewarding pastime of sport shooting and gun collecting. Many Americans strongly believe in their constitutional right to own guns.

Guns can also cause harm, in the hands of criminals and in the hands of an untrained or careless gun owner. The most important element of having a gun is to be properly trained in gun safety, handling, and use. If you own or possess a gun and you don't have such training, or you don't have proper respect for the ability of guns to inflict deadly harm, you can have a gun accident where you, a loved one, or an innocent bystander can be killed or seriously injured.

Make sure you are properly trained, and make sure you handle guns with the degree of respect that these valuable but deadly instruments command.

Legal Reality: One day you may find that you need to use your gun to defend yourself or another person. When and how you do so is a personal decision. Be aware that when you use a gun in such a situation, you set in motion a complicated legal process. Whenever you shoot at someone, you risk going to jail. Two things are likely to happen if you shoot someone: you will be arrested, and you will be sued by the person you shoot or that person's family. This does not mean you shouldn't use your gun to defend yourself or others, or that you will be found guilty and sent to prison, or that you will lose in a civil suit. However, understand that these things may happen when you pull the trigger.

The words of the law, especially regarding self-defense, leave many grey areas. What is "reasonable" and what is unreasonable is subject to interpretation. There is no way to know for certain in advance what kind of behavior your jury will find "reasonable." Juries base their decisions not only on the law, but on who the plaintiff is, who the defendant is, and who the lawyers are. Random outcomes and improper outcomes are not uncommon. Carefully following the law is the best way to protect yourself, but no outcome is certain.

If you are sued in civil court, the burden of proof that the plaintiff must overcome in order to obtain a money judgement against you is "the preponderance of the evidence." This is a much lower burden of proof than the criminal prosecutor's burden of "beyond a reasonable doubt." Even if you are found not guilty of any crime, you could still lose in a civil suit to the person you shoot or his or her family.

How Does Federal Law Relate to California Law?

Federal law is the law of the United States. Both federal law and California law apply to people in California. You must follow both sets of laws.

In general, federal law carries harsher punishments for violations than California law. If you are arrested for an offense that can be charged under either federal or California law, the district attorney and the United States attorney can decide whether to prosecute you under state or federal law. It's their choice.

Both federal and California law apply to people who have guns in California. You must follow both sets of laws.

Are Guns Required to Be Registered?

Except for assault weapons, there is no requirement that guns be "registered." However, the California Legislature has imposed a requirement that has almost the same effect as gun registration: Before most guns in California can be transferred to you, you must fill out a dealer's record of sale (DROS) form or a law enforcement firearms transfer (LEFT) form, which are sent to the DOJ and to local law enforcement agencies. When handguns are transferred, copies of these forms are kept on file by the DOJ in Sacramento.

163

If you already possess a gun that is not an assault weapon, however, you don't have to register it.

What Is a Licensed Gun Dealer?

To be a licensed gun dealer under California law, you need a total of five licenses and certificates:[1]

1. A federal firearms license (FFL).

2. A city or county business license.

3. A valid seller's permit issued by the State Board of Equalization.

4. A certificate of eligibility from the DOJ.

5. A city or county retail firearms dealer license.

You also need to be listed in the DOJ's centralized list of gun dealers. There are numerous additional California laws that apply to gun dealers, most of which are contained in Sections 12070 through 12084. Federal and local laws add additional requirements. After becoming licensed, a gun dealer must follow all applicable laws carefully; a violation can be a misdemeanor, and in certain cases, a felony.

No person licensed under federal law may transfer a gun in California to another person licensed under federal law whose licensed premises are located in California, unless the transferee presents proof that he or she has the five licenses and certificates described above or proof that he or she is exempt from this requirement.[2]

Penalties for Unlawfully Brandishing a Gun

If you draw or exhibit any gun in a "rude, angry, or threatening manner" in the presence of another person, or if you use a gun in any fight or quarrel, *except in self-defense or in defense of another,* you are guilty of a misdemeanor that carries a minimum three month jail term. It doesn't matter whether the gun is loaded, whether the other person actually sees you brandish the gun, or whether you actually intend to injure the other person.[3]

After your first conviction for this offense, you can't have a gun for 10 years; after your second conviction, you can never have a gun again.[4]

If you unlawfully brandish a gun in the presence of an occupant of a motor vehicle that is on a public street or highway (such as pointing a gun at another driver while you are driving), you are guilty of a felony/misdemeanor. Additionally, if you are convicted of brandishing a gun from your motor vehicle, the court will order that your vehicle be seized and sold.[5]

How Must You Store Your Gun Around Children?

Rule for Storing Guns: If you keep any loaded gun in a place where a child can possibly get to it, you must either use a locking device or keep it in a locked container.

Definitions which apply to this rule:[6]

- ❏ A "loaded gun" has the same meaning as for the loaded gun law (see page 41).

- ❏ A "child" means a person under 14 years of age.

- ❏ A "locking device" is a device which temporarily prevents a gun from firing.

- ❏ A "locked container" means a secure container which is fully enclosed and locked by a padlock, key lock, combination lock, or similar locking device.

Improper Storage Causing Serious Injury or Death: You are guilty of a a felony/misdemeanor, including a fine of up to $10,000, if:[7]

1. You keep a loaded gun at any place under your control, and

2. You know or reasonably should know that a child is likely to get access to the gun without the permission of the child's parent or legal guardian, and

3. A child gets access to the gun and causes death or great bodily injury to himself, herself, or any other person.

Improper Storage Causing Minor Injury or Brandishing: You are guilty of a misdemeanor if:[8]

1. You keep a loaded gun at any place under your control, and

2. You know or reasonably should know that a child is likely to get access to the gun without the permission of the child's parent or legal guardian, and

3. A child gets access to the gun and causes minor injury (injury other than great bodily injury) to himself, herself, or any other person, *or*

4. A child gets access to the gun and exhibits it in a public place, or brandishes it in a threatening way, or uses it in a fight.

Exceptions to Gun Storage Laws: You are not guilty of criminal storage of a gun, even if someone is injured or killed, if any of the following is true:[9]

❑   The child obtained the gun because someone entered the premises illegally (such as the child breaking into your house).

❑ The gun was kept in a locked container or in a location where a reasonable person would believe it was secure.

❑ The gun was equipped with a locking device.

❑ The gun was carried on your person, or so close to you that you could reach it and use it as easily as if you were carrying it.

❑ The person keeping the gun was a peace officer or a member of the armed forces or national guard, and the child obtained the gun during, or incidental to, the performance of the person's duties.

❑ The child gets and/or shoots the gun in a lawful act of self-defense, or the defense of another person.

❑ Based on the facts and circumstances, the person keeping the gun could not have reasonably expected a child to come onto the premises. (This is not based on what *you* expected, but what the average, reasonable person in your situation would expect.)

Humane Treatment of Grieving Parents

Prosecution: If a parent or legal guardian violates these gun storage laws, and that parent or guardian's child is injured or dies in an accidental shooting, the district attorney must take into account the impact of the injury or death on the parent or guardian when deciding whether to prosecute. The California Legislature has stated that a parent or guardian whose child is injured or dies in an accidental shooting should only be prosecuted if the parent or guardian behaved in a grossly negligent manner, or if other flagrant circumstances exist.[10]

Arrest: If a parent or legal guardian violates these gun storage laws, and that parent or guardian's child is injured or dies in an accidental shooting, the police may not arrest the parent or guardian until at least seven days after the accidental shooting. Law enforcement officers are encouraged by the Legislature to consider the health status of a child who has suffered great bodily injury, and to delay the arrest of that child's parent or guardian while the child remains on life-support or is in critical condition.[11]

Encouragement to Take Gun Safety Course: If you took a firearm safety training course *before* you bought your gun, and a child later gets the gun in violation of this law, the district attorney must take the training course into account when deciding whether to prosecute you. The fact that you took the course is a "mitigating factor," which means that it lessens your responsibility for the crime.[12]

If you keep a gun in a place where a child can get access to it, and the child injures or kills someone with the gun, you can go to prison.

Obliteration of Identification Marks

If you change, alter, remove, or obliterate (destroy) an identification mark on any gun, without first getting the permission of the DOJ, you are guilty of a felony. Identification marks include the name of the gun maker, model, manufacturer's number, or other identification mark, including numbers and marks assigned by the DOJ.[13]

If you possess, buy, receive, offer for sale, or transfer a gun with a changed, altered, removed, or obliterated identification mark, when you have knowledge of the change, alteration, removal, or obliteration, you are guilty of a misdemeanor.[14]

The DOJ, upon request, will assign a number to any pistol or revolver on which the identification mark has been obliterated. It is okay to place or stamp your own identification mark on a gun, as long as your stamp does not affect the other identification marks on the gun.[15]

Are You Liable if You Have a Gun Accident?

Criminal Liability: If you fire a gun in a grossly negligent manner which could result in the injury or death of a person, you are guilty of a felony/misdemeanor. The handling of guns calls for a high degree of care, and criminal charges are often filed when a gun accident results in someone's injury or death (and such charges can be filed even if no one is hurt by the careless shot). Examples of gross negligence are pointing a gun without checking to see if it is loaded, and handling and shooting a gun in a place where it is likely to injure a person.[16]

Civil Liability: Any time you have any kind of accident, you are liable to any person you injure if you were *negligent*. You are negligent when you do not use "due care," which is the standard of care required for the activity in which you are engaged. For example, when you are driving a car, you are using due care when you are driving in the same manner any capable driver is expected to. Due care in dry weather may be 50 miles per hour for a certain road. If you drive the same road at 50 miles per hour in a nighttime storm, however, you may not be using due care. If you cause an accident, you will be liable to the injured party(ies) for your negligence. Guns are no different. You must use the standard of care appropriate for the handling of dangerous instruments such as guns, and you are liable to anyone you injure if you are negligent.

When Can the Police Confiscate Your Gun?

After the following crimes, your gun and/or ammunition may be declared a "nuisance" and confiscated by the police:[17]

- ❑ Guns carried in violation of the concealed gun law (Section 12025).

- ❑ Illegal guns and ammunition, such as short-barreled shotguns and explosive bullets (Section 12020).

- ❑ Guns possessed by someone who is in a class of persons who are prohibited from having a gun, such as a convicted felon (Sections 12021 and 12021.1).

- ❑ Handguns and ammunition unlawfully possessed by a minor (Section 12101).

- ❑ Guns used in any misdemeanor or felony (except violations of the Fish and Game Code), or in attempts to commit a misdemeanor or felony, after the gun owner has been convicted.

If you are arrested and your gun is confiscated, and you are later found not guilty of any crime, some courts will refuse to order the police to return your gun even though you have not committed a crime. Discuss with your lawyer whether there is a procedure available to have your gun returned to you.

Police officers and other law enforcement officers may also temporarily confiscate guns after certain family violence incidents. The police are required to give you a receipt after taking the guns. Ask the officers and see Section 12028.5 for details on how you can have your guns returned to you.

Gun Laws Related to Carrying Knives

People who carry knives can run into problems when they possess or attempt to buy a gun. If you carry a knife, be aware that a conviction for illegally carrying your knife can restrict your right to have a gun (in addition to the punishment for the knife conviction). A conviction for illegally carrying a knife into a government building, for example, will restrict you from having a gun for 10 years. And a felony conviction for carrying a concealed dirk or dagger will prevent you from having a gun forever.

Be sure you know the state laws on knives. The most commonly violated California knife law is the law against carrying a concealed dirk or dagger. Carrying a dirk or dagger concealed on your person is a felony/misdemeanor.[18]

A dirk or dagger is any knife or other instrument, with or without a handguard, that is capable of ready use as a stabbing weapon that may inflict great bodily injury or death. *This definition is new in 1996 and makes it much easier for a knife to be considered a dirk or dagger.*

A knife carried in a sheath which is worn openly suspended from your waist is not considered concealed for the purpose of this particular law (however, cities and counties often have laws that restrict the open carrying of a knife in a sheath). Note that this book does *not* contain all laws related to the carrying of knives.

Many cities and counties have laws that restrict the carrying of knives. If you want to carry a knife, make sure you learn the knife laws for each city and county in which you will carry your knife, as well as the state laws on knives.

Endnotes

1. Penal Code § 12071(a)(1).

2. Penal Code § 12072(f).

3. Penal Code § 417; People v. Kirk (1986) 192 Cal.App.3d Supp. 15, Supp. 19; People v. McKinzie (1986) 179 Cal.App.3d 789, 794; People v. Norton (1978) 80 Cal.App.3d Supp. 14, Supp. 26.

4. Penal Code §§ 12021(c), 12021(a)(2), 12001.6(c).

5. Penal Code §§ 417.3, 246.1.

6. Penal Code §§ 12035(a), 12026.2(d).

7. Penal Code §§ 12035(b)(1), (d)(1), 12022.7(d).

8. Penal Code §§ 12035(b)(2), (d)(2), 417.

9. Penal Code § 12035(c).

10. Penal Code § 12035(e).

11. Penal Code § 12035(f).

12. Penal Code § 12035(g).

13. Penal Code § 12090.

14. Penal Code § 12094.

15. Penal Code §§ 12092, 12093.

16. Penal Code § 246.3; 2 Witkin & Epstein, *California Criminal Law 2d*, § 523.

17. Penal Code §§ 12028, 12029.

18. Penal Code § 12020(a), (c)(24), (d).

Notes

Significant Changes From 1996 to 1997

Page 7   New waiting periods.

Page 12   Added Basic Firearms Safety Certificate exception #16.

Page 25   New federal prohibited group: persons convicted of a Domestic Violence Misdemeanor.

Page 26   New procedure for restoring gun rights within 10-year period after qualifying misdemeanor. Through page 27.

Page 39   New definition of "loaded gun."

Page 41   Picture caption change—new definition of "loaded gun."

Page 63   New penalties for concealed gun law and loaded gun law. Penalties added and made uniform. Through page 66.

Page 72   New federal school zone law integrated into Schools and Colleges section. Through page 74.

Page 106   Two additional rules added for prohibited people who use a gun in an emergency.

Page 121   Added local ban on sale of Saturday Night Specials/Junk guns.

Page 148   Added warning about modifying guns from *Dingman* assault weapon case.

Page 159   New penalty for wrongfully transferring a gun that is later used in a felony.

Significant Changes From 1995 to 1996

Page 7   New waiting periods.

Page 8   New transfer fee and comments.

Page 12   Added Basic Firearms Safety Certificate exception #15.

Page 19   Additional misdemeanors added to 10-year list. Through page 20.

Page 47   New definition of prohibited person in #3, bottom of page.

Page 49   New definition of prohibited person in #1, top of page.

Page 56   Added exception for gun buy-back programs.

Page 72   New exceptions for K-12 school zone law.

Page 84   CCW issuing agencies can charge an annual license fee.

Page 125   New definition of armor-piercing bullets.

Page 137   Added missing numbering to assault weapon list.

Page 144   Expanded discussion of local assault weapon laws.

Page 151   Only long curios and relics may be transferred freely.

Page 155   Only long curios and relics may be transferred freely.

Page 171   New definition of "dirk or dagger."

Order Form

✉ **Mail Orders:** Send this order form with payment enclosed to:

Gun Law Press
P.O. Box 641369
Los Angeles, CA 90064

Please send me the following books:

How to Own a Gun and Stay Out of Jail

Quantity

_____ California - 1997 edition @ $9.95 each★

_____ California - 1998 edition @ $9.95 each★
(available in December 1997)

★Please add $0.89 sales tax and $2.11 shipping for a total of $12.95 per book.

Allow 2-3 weeks for delivery.
Books will be shipped to California addresses only.

This is your mailing label—please print neatly:

Name:_____

(Company:)_____

Street:_____

City, St., Zip:_____

How to Own a Gun
&
Stay Out of Jail

CALIFORNIA EDITION

1998 Supplement

This supplement covers California laws passed during the 1996-1997 legislative session. These laws take effect on January 1, 1998. No significant federal laws that affect gun owners have been passed since the printing of the 1997 edition. Remember that new, additional laws can be passed when the legislatures reconvene, and can take effect immediately if passed as "urgency" laws.

How to Use This Supplement: Read through the supplement to see what has changed in the past year. You may wish to mark the pages that have changed for easy reference.

Page 7   Handgun "Registration" for New Residents and Licensed Collectors Importing C&R

If you move to California and bring handguns, you must register the guns with the DOJ within 60 days. You are a "personal handgun importer" if you meet all of the following 6 requirements:

1.   You own a handgun which you acquired outside of California, and which was not acquired from a California gun

dealer who followed the California waiting period, background check, forms, and other requirements.

2. You move to California after January 1, 1998 to live here as a resident, and you intend to possess the handgun here. Residency is determined by the same test used for driver's licenses (see Vehicle Code Section 12505 for details). Members of the U.S. armed forces are residents when they are discharged from active service in California.

3. While a resident of California, you did not previously file a report with the DOJ about this handgun.

4. The handgun is not an illegal gun (see Page 117) or an assault weapon under California law (see Page 136).

5. You are 18 years of age or older.

6. You are not a California-licensed gun dealer or a federally-licensed gun manufacturer or importer.

If you meet the above requirements, you must do one of the following within 60 days of bringing the handgun to California:

❑   Mail or deliver a report to the DOJ giving information about yourself and the handgun you imported. The form for the report will be available from gun dealers and law enforcement agencies.

❑   Sell or transfer the handgun to another person, to a gun dealer, or to a sheriff or police department, following the rules for transferring a gun in California (see Chapter 9).

Remember, whenever you bring a gun to a law enforcement agency for any reason, give prior notice to the agency that you are doing so, unload the gun, and transport all handguns and assault weapons in a locked container.

Licensed Collectors: A federally-licensed collector whose licensed premises are in California, and who takes possession of a curio or relic handgun outside of California, must file a report with the DOJ on a DOJ form within 5 days of transporting that handgun into California.

A violation of either of these laws by a person with no previous convictions is a misdemeanor; a violation by a person with certain prior convictions is a felony. However, if you violate these laws by missing the 60-day or 5-day grace periods, you will not be charged with a crime if your violation is only discovered when you file the report.[1]

Page 7   Waiting Period—
Electronic Forms System In Place

All California gun dealers now transmit gun purchaser or transferee information to the DOJ via computer or telephone. The waiting period for all guns is 10 days (actually 10 24-hour periods); there is no time added for mailing.

Page 26   Restoring Your Gun Rights—
Relief from Misdemeanor 10-Year Ban

The rule of the *Evans* court case referred to at the top of page 27 has been written into the Penal Code at Section 12021(c)(3).

Page 32   Ammunition Sales to Minors—
No Handgun Ammunition to Under 21

The minimum age for sales of ammunition or ammunition-related devices has been increased for handgun ammunition. Any person who sells handgun ammunition to a person under 21 years of age is guilty of a misdemeanor. The minimum age for long gun ammunition remains 18. Handgun ammunition means ammunition principally for use in handguns, even though it can also be used in some rifles.[2]

Page 36   Concealed Gun Law—
Now Applies to Vehicle Occupants

The concealed gun law now applies to passengers in vehicles, as well as drivers. Having the vehicle under your control or direction is no longer a requirement.[3]

Page 51 Concealed Gun Law— New Exceptions for Certain Situations

There are three new exceptions that apply to the concealed gun law, but not to the loaded gun law:

- ❑ A person who finds a lost handgun can transport the gun to a law enforcement agency so that the agency can locate the owner or give possession of the gun to the person who found it.

- ❑ A person who finds a handgun can transport it to a law enforcement agency for disposal.

- ❑ A "personal handgun importer" can transport a handgun when selling or transferring the gun to comply with the law.

The exceptions related to transporting the gun to a law enforcement agency require you to give prior notice to the agency that you are bringing the gun to them.[4]

Page 81 Concealed Weapons Licenses— Police Chiefs Issue to City Residents Only

Sheriffs can issue a license to any resident of their county, but police chiefs are now restricted to issuing to residents of their cities. If you wish to apply for a permit, you can apply to your county sheriff, the police chief in the city where you live, or both.[5]

Page 105 Prohibited Persons— New Exception for Guns in Emergencies

A new exception provides an alternative to the rules in *People v. King.* A person prohibited from having a gun can possess a gun if all of the following apply:

1. The person found the gun, or took the gun from someone who was committing a crime against him or her.

2. The person possessed the gun no longer than necessary to deliver the gun to a law enforcement agency.

3. If the person transported the gun to a law enforcement agency to turn it in, he or she gave prior notice to the agency, and transported the gun in a lawful manner.

4. The person is prohibited from having a gun only by Section 12021, and not by Section 12021.1 (serious felonies on page 14), or by Welfare & Institutions Code Sections 8100 or 8103 (mental illness-related restrictions).

At trial, the defendant has the burden of proving that he or she met the above requirements. Another new exception allows a prohibited person to possess ammunition if the person follows the same requirements.[6]

Page 126 Illegal Guns—
Exception for Transporting Guns to Police

You may possess a gun from the list of illegal guns that starts on page 117 if you follow all of the following rules:

1. The gun is not a short-barreled rifle, short-barreled shotgun, or machine gun.

2. You are not in a class of persons who is prohibited from having a gun.

3. You possess the gun no longer than necessary to deliver the gun to a law enforcement agency for disposal.

4. If you transport the gun to a law enforcement agency to turn it in, you give prior notice to the agency, and transport the gun in a lawful manner. The gun must be transported in a locked container. A locked container means a secure container which is fully enclosed and locked by a padlock, key lock, combination lock, or similar locking device.

The same exceptions and requirements apply to the possession of armor-piercing ammunition by a person who found the ammunition, and to the possession of guns with obliterated identification marks.[7]

Page 138 Assault Weapons—
Adding Guns to the List

At the time of this printing, no guns have been added to California's assault weapon list since January 1, 1992. However, recent political activity in this area may result in additional guns being added in the near future. If you have a gun that has characteristics common to assault weapons, but is not currently on the list, make sure you stay current with changes to the list.

Page 140 DOJ Zip Code Correction
The zip code of the California Department of Justice is 94203.

Page 165 Storing Guns Around Children—New Rules
There are two changes to the definitions:

❑ A "child" is now a person under 16 years of age.

❑ A "locking device" means a device designed to prevent a gun from firing and when applied to the gun makes it inoperable.

Improper Storage Causing Minor Injury or Brandishing: Paragraph 4 is modified such that a violation is committed when a child carries the gun to a public place. Exhibiting it is no longer a requirement.

Pursuant to a new Penal Code section, you are guilty of a misdemeanor when a child obtains access to your gun and removes it from the premises where you stored the gun. This new law also provides that your gun will be confiscated. The same set of exceptions apply to this law as to the other gun storage laws.[8]

Page 171 Knives—New "Dirk or Dagger" Exception
The definition of "dirk or dagger" has been changed, so that the following three types of knives are dirks or daggers only when the blade is exposed and locked into position: